To the Limit

TO THE LIMIT

The Meaning of Endurance, from Mexico to the Himalayas

Michael Crawley

BLOOMSBURY SPORT
LONDON · OXFORD · NEW YORK · NEW DELHI · SYDNEY

BLOOMSBURY SPORT
Bloomsbury Publishing Plc
50 Bedford Square, London, WC1B 3DP, UK
29 Earlsfort Terrace, Dublin 2, Ireland

BLOOMSBURY, BLOOMSBURY SPORT and the Diana logo are trademarks of
Bloomsbury Publishing Plc

First published in Great Britain, 2024

For legal purposes the Acknowledgements on p. 259 constitute an extension of this
copyright page

A catalogue record for this book is available from the British Library

Library of Congress Cataloguing-in-Publication data has been applied for

ISBN: HB: 978-1-3994-0342-9; ePUB: 978-1-3994-0345-0; EPDF: 978-1-3994-0343-6

2 4 6 8 10 9 7 5 3 1

Typeset in Deanta Global Publishing Services, Chennai, India
Printed and bound in Great Britain by CPI Group (UK) Ltd, Croydon, CRO 4YY

To find out more about our authors and books visit www.bloomsbury.com
and sign up for our newsletters

To Roslyn, Maddy and Silas.

CONTENTS

1

THRELKELD IN THE RAIN

It is mid-September and the weather in Durham is just starting to turn after a late-summer heatwave. I am training for a 50-mile race in the Lake District and I decide I need at least a little bit of practice on the fells, so I set off at 9 p.m. one evening to drive down to my dad's empty house in Penrith. The sat nav takes me on a crazy single-track detour to avoid roadworks on the A66 and sheets of rain lash the windscreen. I arrive at 11 p.m. and root around in the garden with my torch, looking for the spare key and hoping none of the neighbours see me and call the police.

The next morning I set off from Threlkeld to run a section of the route up to Helvellyn, and the rain still hasn't let up. I run out of the village and make my way up Great Dodd, avoiding the narrow paths which are flowing freely with rainwater. I'm always surprised by how much these climbs sap your energy through a combination of steepness and the soft, wet ground pulling at your feet. I make my way along the ridge to Watson's Dodd and the wind is so strong I have to shield my eyes with my hand. I try to run in the rutted tracks, my feet already so wet the running water is not a problem, but I keep getting blown into the tufty grass to the side of me and having to steady myself.

The hood of my jacket is slapping me repeatedly in the face, and the rain is now so hard and horizontal that I end up inhaling some. My watch beeps to tell me I've run an incredibly slow kilometre and I hit the stop button in frustration. The visibility is still reasonable, though, and I tell myself that it could easily be this bad on the day of the race. I push on, but the conditions just get worse and worse. Soon I can barely see a couple of metres ahead of me and I need to use the OS Maps app on my increasingly soaked phone to confirm where I am. It sounds melodramatic – it's not like I'm clinging to the side of an 8000m peak in the Himalayas with just an ice axe – but when there is almost no visibility, and you've come up into the hills in shorts, and you're drenched to the skin and two hours from your car, and the hail really starts pounding, it can get quite scary.

The thought does frequently occur to me in the course of writing this book: what am I doing? And its attendant question, after twenty or so years of competing in endurance events: what have I done? Why have I devoted so much time to this? To trying to determine the limits to my body? To chasing arbitrary time goals, desperately competing for international vests? Embarking on an anthropological project on the meaning of endurance is an attempt to answer these questions for myself, as well as an opportunity to think about the range of meanings people bring to endurance sports, and the connection between endurance and what it means to be human.

By the time I wend my way back into Threlkeld two hours later, I am streaked with mud from a comical fall and severely humbled by the elements. The rain has eased to a light drizzle, a ray of sunshine has made its tentative way out to turn the fields green and, of course, this all begins to seem like a worthwhile way to spend time again. Perhaps the vulnerability is what we crave, even if to seek it we must, at times, veer uncomfortably close to stupidity. There is something to be learnt, as the poet Devin Kelly puts it, from 'being as far along the edge of yourself as possible.'

Learning to endure and explore limits has, for a long time, been a lens through which to look at life and wider society more generally, and how exactly endurance challenges might relate to what is going on in society more broadly is one of the main themes I want to investigate. On the one hand, these things seem to offer an escape from the pressures of modern life. We lace up our running shoes or jump on our bike, and for a few hours at least we are away from our emails and our phones, and our thoughts are free to wander. People talk of 'stripping things back' and returning to something more simple and profound; of embracing their own vulnerability. On the other hand, though, we have a tendency to think of these activities precisely in the kind of terms we are ostensibly trying to escape – we celebrate individual resilience, the endless drive for productivity, the quantification of ever-more variables, the ranking of individuals in terms of performance. 'The way people play is perhaps more revealing than the way they work,' the anthropologist Victor Turner once wrote. But what happens when the two things start to become indistinguishable?

'Here at Amazon,' reads a pamphlet issued to workers at the online retailer's Tulsa, Oklahoma facility in 2020, 'you will become an industrial athlete. Just like an athlete who trains for an event, industrial athletes need to prepare their bodies to be able to perform their best at work.' The pamphlet, which Amazon say was created 'in error' and was later removed, suggests that workers stretch before and after their shifts, and it contains recommendations about sleep and diet to maximise performance and decrease the likelihood of injury. Distribution centre workers can walk up to 13 miles during a shift and lift a total of 9000kg, it says, before giving the details of several sports massage therapists and physios in the area. Whatever you think about the expectation that workers 'perform their best' for little more than minimum wage, the pamphlet is an example of the increasingly common conflation of work, exercise and endurance.

We can see this happening elsewhere in the corporate world, too. For example, a few years ago Johnson and Johnson, the world's largest healthcare company, launched an initiative called Corporate Athlete Resilience at its Human Performance Institute. This is intended to help its clients' employees manage stress by supporting individuals to 'redefine and strategically leverage stress for growth and improved performance.' Wearable technologies like Fitbit, Garmin and the Apple Watch (more on them in chapter 3) are designed to do something similar, encouraging us to understand the 'stress' of both exercise and work via the same metric. As the sociologist Chris Till writes, 'Exercise and labour are in a process of merging in such a fashion that in a short space of time, the two may seem inseparable.'

If our workplaces increasingly expect us to live like athletes just to cope at work, it is somewhat surprising that we see a simultaneous rise in people entering increasingly extreme endurance events, which are pitched as an escape from work. In Scotland recently, a four-day ultra-distance race charged a £15,499 entry fee for what it described as the first ever 'premium ultra'. It invited participants to 'revel in a luxury wilderness,' supported by Michelin-starred chefs, a 'sporting concierge' and a fitness expert from Porsche. Participants completed trail running sections on Scottish Islands before being whisked between them on speedboats and the event culminated with dinner in a castle hosted by Sir

Ranulph Fiennes. If you've got enough money, it is implied, even endurance can be luxurious.

Many of us now use activity trackers to measure not only the time we spend running, cycling or in the gym, but our whole lives. We want to know how many steps we did when we took our kids to the park and see our 'sleep performance' visualised as a percentage. The 24/7 insights provided by devices like the Whoop strap, which calculates heart rate variability (HRV) using a sensor on your wrist, encourage us to think about 'how strenuous your training *and day* is.' Life itself becomes an endurance test, to be measured with the kind of metrics that used to be the preserve of elite athletes. Even sleep is something to be assessed in terms of productivity.

On platforms like Instagram we are bombarded with messages that make exercise – and the failure to exercise – a personal responsibility. Exercise and endurance are characterised as part of a wider drive towards productivity and the kind of constant self-improvement that spins the wheels of capital. We are exhorted to get up earlier and put in that extra effort to 'Beat yesterday' (Garmin) or be #BetterEveryDay as the hashtag would have it. Even the Samuel Beckett lines – 'Try again. Fail again. Better again' – have become a motivational meme, despite originally appearing in a story entitled 'Worstward Ho!' about gradual and inevitable decline.

If you're reading this and you're a keen runner with a smartphone or wearable fitness device, you're like me: engaged in a process not only of running when we go out of the door, but of creating increasingly valuable data for big companies. We are, then, working in a very literal way. If we post about a run on Instagram, we are creating more value – for ourselves perhaps in some way – but also for the platform. We are engaging in a form of prosumption (simultaneous production and consumption) that reinforces the idea of endurance as an individual, almost narcissistic pursuit: *my* data, *my* mid-run selfie.

This way of thinking means that endurance is seen as a capacity of individual bodies, calculated in terms of hours trained, resting heartrate and minutes of sleep. We see our work as an opportunity to test our endurance , think of our sleep in terms of productivity, and use our leisure time to engage in increasingly extreme endurance challenges. What this does is shift the conversation towards an individual responsibility to perform, making any failure to endure an indication of individual weakness. When did we start to think of endurance in this way? And in what other ways might we think about endurance?

It is especially important to ask these questions right now. Although the pandemic may seem far behind us, many of us are exhausted and balancing multiple stresses. Getting through the series of lockdowns was often characterised as an endurance test, albeit one that was defined primarily by stasis and solitariness. More of us ran than usual during the first lockdown, using a different kind of endurance as a coping mechanism. We ran to shed the anxiety and as a way of keeping going, and to judge from the numbers who take part in races, many of us are still running.

Yet with the increasingly doom-laden reports about climate change and the horizon of 'when things are back to normal after the pandemic' receding ever further, we need to think carefully about how we endure and what endurance means to us. With the challenges we currently face, perhaps our focus on individual endurance is misplaced. Alongside the growth of events like Ironman, which require huge amounts of specialist kit, there is also a lot of interest in endurance cultures that are seen as 'simpler' or more 'natural'.

This is the way Kenyan and Ethiopian endurance runners are often characterised, and it is key to the depiction of people like the Rarámuri runners in Mexico (often referred to as the 'Tarahumara', the name imposed on them by the Spanish) and the Sherpa working with international climbers in Nepal. If there was one thing I sought to emphasise in my book on Ethiopian running it was that the Ethiopian approach may appear less 'scientific', but it is as far from 'simple' as it is possible to get. These kind of depictions tend to start with particular *physiological* characteristics – the tendency to run barefoot, for example, or the adaptations that need to be made for life at altitude – and to build assumptions from there. They rarely ask what it *means* to endure in Eldoret in Kenya or in the Sierra Madre of Mexico, what kind of values are attached to those forms of endurance, or what kind of spiritual or economic importance they might have. I am therefore keen to examine some examples of endurance as a communal process of transformation and as a form of ritual, both in the UK and elsewhere.

How important is it that we consider endurance as movement and that we move together? And how might we create social value through our endurance, rather than just creating monetary value for corporations for whom our run is little more than a series of numbers that can be converted into another series of numbers with £ signs in front of them? Finally, how is the act of enduring and of moving through space changing the ways in which we think about the natural world and our place within it?

I started asking myself these questions when I got back from a 15-month period of ethnographic fieldwork in Ethiopia, where

I lived and trained alongside a group of professional runners. There, I documented an understanding of endurance as a collective experience. To get the best out of themselves in running, and in life, athletes had to be invested in the group. It was important to co-operate with others and share energy expenditure equally in order to improve together. I was woken almost every morning by someone knocking on my door and reminding me that it was time to get up and run, together. 'Running alone is just for health,' I was told. 'To be changed you have to run with others.' The transformative potential of enduring *together* was reiterated constantly.

The majority of academic work on 'endurance' comes from sports science and evolutionary anthropology. For sports scientists the measurement of endurance is done using a set of specific physiological parameters, such as VO_2 max, lactic threshold and running economy. In other words, what is the capacity of your body and its constituent parts? How efficiently do your lungs process oxygen? How good are your muscles at absorbing the oxygen that is carried in your blood? For evolutionary anthropologists, who are often interested in the lives of people who must expend energy moving from place to place, or whose access to food depends to a certain extent on physical activity, the ability to endure is similarly measured in terms of efficiency: how many calories were burned on that hunt compared to the nutritional benefits provided by the meat that came from it? This characterises endurance practices like persistence hunting, in which you essentially run after your prey until you wear it out, as exercises in probability and calculation (calories in versus calories out).

For a social anthropologist like myself, it feels like there are some very important questions that are not being explored. For instance, how does increasing access to data change how people think about their potential and their relationship to their body? What does hunting by gradually chasing down a deer over many hours of running actually mean to people? Does hunting in this way carry a greater significance than shooting something with an arrow?

As the sociologist Lindsey Freeman points out, there have been many attempts to define what 'we' in the West are doing wrong in relation to the more 'authentic' endurance practices that can be observed in other parts of the world. Indeed, I have been involved in this myself, when I sought to distil some of what is unique about Ethiopian running into my first book, *Out of Thin Air*. It is also clear that in an ever-more interconnected world, practices and ideas about endurance travel rapidly: I found the Nike slogan, 'Go hard or go home', etched on to the weekly training plan of the girls at the Mira Rai Initiative in Gokarna outside Kathmandu in Nepal. The Rarámuri runners in Mexico are now just as likely to run in straightforward races (*marathones*) as they are to run in their traditional *rarájipari* contests, which involve two teams guiding a wooden ball for endless laps, often for over 100km. Many of the *rarájipari* contests that do happen are now organised by cultural heritage organisations and sponsored by outsiders keen for the practice to continue, rather than initiated by the Rarámuri themselves.

By looking at a range of endurance practices I want to find out what motivates us to do hard things, how those motivations differ around the world and what we might learn if we consider a more holistic approach. However, I want to avoid making the kind of stark 'us' and 'them' or 'West versus the rest' comparisons that many recent accounts of the Rarámuri, climbing Sherpas or hunter-gatherers like the Hadza in Tanzania have relied on. Rather, as the anthropologist Anna Tsing puts it, I am interested in exploring the ways in which 'cultures are continually co-produced in the interactions I call "friction": the awkward, unusual, unstable and creative qualities of interconnection across difference.'

I am aware, though, that many of these interactions with 'cultures of endurance' can be about extracting some quality or essence, or they are geared towards marketing, for instance barefoot running shoes or chia seeds, both of which were popularised as a result of interest in the 'secrets' of the Rarámuri. There has also been a tendency to lay claim to particular kinds of expertise, for instance in the various projects that sought to 'break' the two-hour marathon. In these endeavours, the emphasis is usually on the technology involved, as opposed to the athletes themselves. In 2019, I remember watching the Ineos 1.59 event, where Eliud Kipchoge did, incredibly, manage to run under two hours, and feeling a mixture of awe and ambivalence. Something about the lasers, the incredibly straight roads and the military precision of the pacemakers made the event seem sterile. In an Edinburgh pub that evening I was struck by how many people were talking about the event, but something about the way Kipchoge's success was attributed primarily to various corporations and technologies left me feeling cold.

The 15 months I spent living and running alongside marathon runners in Ethiopia taught me that far from what people normally assume about East African athletes – that running comes 'naturally' or that success derives almost automatically from the advantages of genetics or altitude – there is a huge amount of expertise about endurance running in Ethiopia. This can look a little different to Western sports science. It is less about lab testing and utilising data, and more about creating a balance in training between different kinds of environmental conditions and learning to share energy with others.

For a long time African knowledge, in particular, has been seen by the West as intuitive, superstitious and practical, but not scientific and therefore as less valuable. I think it is important to emphasise that the way in which Ethiopian and Kenyan runners approach their training, for example, *is* highly scientific. The historian Britt Rusert has coined the term 'fugitive science', broadening the definition of science to include other kinds of embodied empirical practice. East African runners, and populations like the Rarámuri and the Hadza, have often been approached by researchers primarily as a source of physiological data, rather than being taken seriously as people with in-depth knowledge about endurance. For example, it was possible to watch most of the coverage of the attempt to break the two-hour marathon without finding out about the coach who has guided Kipchoge's entire career, Patrick Sang, a Kenyan whose coaching philosophy extends far beyond the track and who Kipchoge himself refers to as a 'life coach'. Sadly, though, there are clear and obvious reasons why Kipchoge's transcendent running has often been framed primarily in terms of technological progress, whether in the form of carbon fibre shoes, new kinds of energy products or live glucose monitoring: all of these make people money.

Lindsey Freeman describes watching the coverage of the world's first sub-two-hour marathon in her playful handbook, *Running*. 'I was drifting around bored in a sea of experts on aerodynamics, nutritionists, timing technologies and special carbon fibre shoes,' she writes. 'I felt that the packaging of the event and its media coverage were drowning out everything I loved about running' – sentiments which matched my own exactly. It was through focusing on the pacemakers that she found meaning in the event, and it was them Kipchoge first spoke to after he crossed the line, thanking them for 'sharing their energy'. As Freeman notes, 'What we are learning, again and again, is that we cannot do this alone.'

Wittingly or unwittingly, expertise is often appropriated in this way and often with the backing of global brands. When I ran the mountainous Sindhupalchok ultra-marathon in Nepal I ran against (and a long way behind) an experienced Nepali runner called Arjun Rai, with whom I was able to chat, with the help of a translator (more on this in chapter 9). Later in the year he was signed by the North Face Adventure Team, running (and winning) the Fishtail 100km race in his first appearance for the brand. Afterwards he thanked them on Instagram, saying, 'I learn about race strategy and nutrition for the first time.' This is perhaps an awkward translation of what he said by whoever is now managing his social media, but nevertheless it seemed to me like he already knew quite a lot about race strategy and nutrition when he beat me by more than three hours. It would be like Frida Kahlo, who never received formal training, attending an oil painting workshop when her career was already established and thanking them for finally teaching her how to paint.

In this book I set out to present endurance expertise, wherever in the world it is to be found, in its own terms, rather than as 'secrets' we can take away or products we can buy. Instead of seeing it as radically different to our own way of 'doing' endurance, I think it is possible to identify a great many similarities. I also want to rehabilitate an approach to endurance sport that emphasises learning through experience, or discovery through practice, as opposed to the application of 'scientific' principles. As Steve Magness, author of *The Science of Running*, has pointed out on X, 'In the exercise world, the science/research is generally 10-20 years behind what the best coaches are doing.' This is a fascinating admission from a top sports scientist and I would be tempted to go further and say that it is not only the best coaches who are responsible for the major innovations, but the athletes themselves.

The history of training for long-distance running is one of citizen scientists innovating through experiments carried out largely on themselves, where the methodology usually involved doing huge amounts of running. These figures were often considered dangerous mavericks and reactions to them ranged from suspicion of the 'Flying Finn' Paavo Nurmi, the first runner to regularly carry a stop-watch which helped him break 22 world records in the 1920s, to incredulity at Emil Zátopek's extreme interval training, which was seen as crazy at the time, but enabled him to become the only person in history to win the 5000m, 10,000m and marathon at a single Olympic Games, in Helsinki in 1952. Given Steve Magness's assessment, to approach the sport primarily through the analysis of things like lactic thresholds and heart rate zones is akin to focusing on the art historians rather than the artists themselves.

The most surprising thing to me about Chris McDougall's best-selling account of the Rarámuri, *Born to Run*, is the extent of the focus on what they had on their feet compared with the cultural and spiritual significance of running. Given the emphasis we place in the West on the gear we run in, and especially on shoe technology, this isn't that surprising, but to stretch the analogy above further, it's a little like asking a writer about the pen they write with, not their literary craft or relationship to the characters they create. When I spoke to runners in Ethiopia who ran in sandals or barefoot, their explanation was always simple (they couldn't afford running shoes) and they always said they would prefer to run in Nike or Adidas trainers if they could (who wouldn't).

Until I started writing this book the world of endurance sport I was familiar with was relatively limited. I was interested in getting faster at running races of between 5 and 42km, primarily on roads, and with the kind of carefully planned and executed training that allows you to do so. Yet even the culture of this type of distance running has changed markedly in the UK in the last 50 years, as I discovered in trying to recreate my coach's old training regime from when he was running for Gateshead Harriers.

On 16 January 1982, Max ran the Orange Bowl Marathon in Miami in 2.14.46, a time that would have been good enough for fourth in the British rankings 30 years later. In March 1982, he stood nervously by the track at Gateshead Stadium waiting for the team for the National 12-stage Road Relays to be announced. His was the very last name on a team that included Olympic medallist and multiple world record holder Brendan Foster, Charlie Spedding, who would go on to win the bronze medal in the Olympic marathon in 1984, and other top internationals like Dennis Coates, who was ninth in the Olympic steeplechase.

Max lent me two hardback National Rail diaries that represented two years of training, the annual mileage neatly calculated on the final pages at 9,037 miles over two years. The diaries are relatively short on description, with the prize for most commonly used adjective going overwhelmingly to 'tired', with only occasional elaboration ('tired – knackered actually'). Beyond times run and distance covered the only other information given is who he was running with – often he would meet Charlie and a few others at Brendan's house on a Sunday morning, and most of the harder sessions were with a group.

The diaries are testament to a belief in the value of patience and hard work in spite of a busy job – when necessary, Max claims to have squeezed a ten-mile run and a sandwich into a one-hour lunch break – but they also show how little has changed about serious distance running training over the years except that fewer people seem willing to train in this way. The success of the Ingebritsen brothers in Norway has led to an interest in the 'double threshold' training they do – two hard training sessions on the same day. However, Max was doing this in 1981 on the advice of his coach Alan Storey, and when I trained for marathons I would copy the training days that consisted of a hard four-mile run in the morning and the same run in the evening. I quickly learnt how well it worked and enjoyed replicating this training pattern, because it allowed me to connect to a no-nonsense culture of running in the North East that has never been the same since. It is safe to say that I have always been drawn to random acts of endurance, although that is definitely not the case for everyone.

When I was travelling around India in 2010, I made a friend whilst trekking in Ladakh. Rowan was a former semi-professional cyclist and had come across a company that hired mountain bikes to tourists before dropping them off at the top of the highest motorable road in the world in a Jeep, so that they could ride the 40km descent back into town. He had persuaded them to let him hire a bike and ride *up* as well as down, which would involve gaining several thousand metres of altitude in a short space of time, peaking at just under 6000m above sea level. In order to do this he had had to sign a special disclaimer, which definitely contained multiple mentions of the word 'death'. Did I want to join him?

Whilst the others recovered from our nine-day trek by visiting a donkey sanctuary, Rowan and I rode uphill for several consecutive hours, gradually becoming more disoriented by the thin air and struggling to keep our bikes moving forwards on the gravelly surface. The only traffic that day came in the form of military convoys that had to squeeze carefully past us on the single-track road, but when we mistakenly peered over the edge as we made our slow way from hairpin bend to hairpin bend, we could see the carcasses of trucks and buses that had got these calculations slightly wrong.

We finally arrived at the top of the pass and were just about able to pose weakly by a brightly painted road sign, draped with prayer flags and with the altitude reading marked on it, when I started to feel too sick to stand up straight. 'Better get you back down,' I remember Rowan saying, before he took off on the descent. I had just enough cognitive capacity left to decide that I wasn't going to try to match the descending skills of someone who had ridden professionally and luckily, minutes later, as Rowan raced off into the distance, I felt better as soon as I had dropped down a few hundred metres of altitude.

*   *   *

If it seems like there has been something of an explosion of interest in endurance challenges in recent years, this pales in comparison to some periods of history. For a couple of decades in the mid to late 19th century, for example, there was a sport so popular that tens of thousands of spectators crowded venues in America and England for an entire week. Such was its significance that a contest in 1879 marked the first instance of electric lighting being put to popular use, representing a serious investment on behalf of the organiser and demonstrating the extreme fascination with the event.

That same year, Gilmore's Garden in New York was already at capacity three hours before a match began. So many enthusiasts tried to crowd in that when the head of the local police, Captain Alexander Williams, ordered the hall to be cleared it marked one of the most significant moments of civic unrest in New York's history. Later in the competition a balcony collapsed under the weight of the wealthier spectators, seriously injuring at least nine people, and yet the show, as they say, went on. What sport could spark such frenzied attention? The answer is walking.

One of the earliest examples of an endurance challenge capturing the popular imagination came in 1809, when Robert Barclay Allardice, a Scottish aristocrat, made a bet that he could walk one mile every hour for 1000 consecutive hours, a format strikingly similar to the modern 'backyard ultra'. If he did so, his friend James Webster would pay him 1000 guineas, at a time when the average British worker earned one guinea a week. In 1818 a man named Josiah Eaton walked a quarter mile every 15 minutes for six weeks, whilst in 1877 William Gale walked 4000 quarter-miles in 4000 consecutive 10-minute periods (nearly 28 days), a schedule which allowed only minutes of sleep at a time.

All of this walking was a lucrative business, with the stars of 'pedestrianism' capable of earning the equivalent of hundreds of thousands of dollars at a time. Madame 'Ada' Anderson, for example, made the equivalent of $162,000 for walking a quarter-mile every 15 minutes for 1000 consecutive hours in Mozart Garden in Brooklyn, New York, at the end of the 19th century. The most popular format was the six-day race, which attracted people from all walks of life, from wealthy businessmen and politicians to the homeless, whose ticket entitled them to a roof for a week. Total gate receipts from these contests could be close to a million dollars.

As Matthew Algeo's brilliant book on the subject, *Pedestrianism: When Watching People Walk was America's Favourite Spectator Sport*, makes clear, everyone had an opinion on the 'pedestrianism' phenomenon, from writers and journalists to politicians and priests, and yet it was hard to put a finger on what the attraction was. 'Watching half-dead men stagger in circles for days on end might strike the reader as monotonous, if not outright boring,' writes Algeo, and yet there was something 'oddly captivating' about it. 'It was like watching a NASCAR race in super-slow motion: hypnotic, mesmerising, with the promise of imminent catastrophe.'

It is perhaps significant that at the time both America and the UK were very much walking nations. As Algeo puts it, whilst the 1% might have travelled sitting down, the 99% walked. And yet it was also a moment in which this was under threat from mechanisation. As Walter Bernstein wrote in the *Virginia Quarterly Review*, 'It seemed as though the muscles of the nation were making one final, vast, collective effort before being replaced by the internal combustion engine.'

There was also, it should be remembered, very little else to do in terms of recreation in the late 19th century. On both sides of the Atlantic there were deep-seated work ethics rooted in Protestant and Evangelical Christianity combined with the new capitalist imperatives of profit and growth, and these prevented the emergence of almost all kinds of recreation. Perhaps it was the sheer work-like nature of long-distance walking that made it the exception that captured the imagination of the public.

In 1879 a writer for the *Brooklyn Daily Eagle* predicted what a 'walking match of a hundred years from now' might look like. The 146th international contest for the pedestrian championship, they wrote, would see 'Shang Smith' retaining the belt for walking an astonishing 1095 miles in six days before an 'aggregate attendance of two million', taking home $98,762.52 for his troubles. In fact, six-day racing was effectively banned only 10 years later, at least in New York, when 'any contest of skill, speed or endurance which shall continue for more than 48 hours' was made illegal. The last great 'pedestrianism' record therefore stood for over 100 years. In 1888 George Littlewood set a six-day record with 623 miles, a total that stood until the great ultra-runner Yiannis Kouros, who doubted that such a distance was possible, somehow covered 635 miles in six days in 1984.

We can trace the history of many concerns that still dominate endurance sports to this era of six-day racing. The first medical studies on endurance athletes were published in the *Lancet* at this time, with a focus on what they consumed during contests, from beef tea and egg yolks to 'sea moss farina' (a seaweed-based supplement and gelatine substitute that's still available today), champagne and brandy diluted with water. This early 'sports science' was accompanied by the first real technological innovations, which came not from companies like Nike and Supersapiens, but from a cobbler named James Welsher, who designed a shoe with a built-in spring some 200 years before the American sportswear giant. The famous jeweller, Tiffany & Co, produced the first pedometer around the same time.

In other ways, though, how we approach endurance sport now is completely different. Perhaps the closest equivalent to six-day racing we have in the UK at the moment is the 268-mile Spine Race, which follows the Pennine Way from Edale in the Peak District to Kirk Yetholm in the Scottish Borders. Rather than attracting those desperate enough to suffer through days of sleepless walking for the lure of serious prize money, the winter version of the Spine Race costs competitors almost £1200 to enter. There might be a few spectators on the route, but most will be content to watch this suffering unfold from afar, 'dot-watching' on their phones.

A few decades after the pedestrianism craze, it was not endurance walking but dancing that captured the public mood in America, with the dance marathon industry employing around 20,000 people as promoters, masters of ceremonies, judges, trainers, contestants and medical professionals. Like six-day walking events, dance marathons had a fraught relationship with the law, with many states attempting to make them illegal or restricting endurance-based entertainment to 12 hours out of 24.

In one early dance marathon the contestants had to go to extraordinary lengths to circumvent these laws, dancing out of the Audubon Ballroom in New York into a waiting van. Here they (somehow) continued to dance whilst being conveyed to the Edgewater Ferry, where they could continue to dance on the deck across the Hudson River to New Jersey, where they hoped to find a more welcoming jurisdiction. Rejected again, they returned briefly to a flat in Harlem before travelling on to the Cygnet

Athletic Club in Connecticut. Finally, after 69 hours of continuous dancing, the police arrived and compelled the last-remaining couple to stop.

Eventually attempts were made to regulate dance marathons (most notably by the not very fun sounding National Endurance Amusement Association), but these were only ever partially successful and the practice remained controversial. With the introduction of regular rest and meal breaks, later dance marathons could go on for weeks at a time. In 1931, for example, a couple called the McGreevys won a show in Miami after dancing for 1264 hours. The prize was $700 and the opportunity to sleep for 10 hours on Beauty Rest mattresses in the window of a sponsoring furniture company, a well-earned rest that was observed by a crowd of curious onlookers.

Because they lasted so long, the marathons became curiously domestic scenes. Depending on what time the audience arrived, they might see the dancers eating dinner at a table raised high enough for them to continue 'dancing' or they might see them having a shave or a pedicure, all on the stage. To make watching people dance (and often it resembled more of an agonised shuffle) for days and weeks on end entertaining, proceedings were interspersed with various other forms of amusement, including mock (and sometimes real) weddings, 'sprints' around the arena and 'zombie treadmills' where contestants would race whilst blindfolded and tied together.

It seems clear that one of the things that drew people to watch dance marathons was a kind of culture of cruelty. As the actress and dancer June Havoc put it at the time, 'Our degradation was entertainment; sadism was sexy, masochism was talent.' Coins would be thrown on to the stage after songs demanding more vigorous dancing and onlookers would watch contestants scrabble for them. According to the promoter and publicist Richard Elliott, 'People came to see them die. That's an over-statement. But they came to see them suffer and to see when they were going to fall down. They wanted to see if their favourites were going to make it. That was all part of it. It was Depression entertainment.'

According to Carol Martin's book on the subject, dance marathons enacted a kind of commentary on America during the 1930s. 'Dreary repetition punctuated by crises was a good metaphor of the seemingly endless depression,' she writes. Marathons performed a kind of social Darwinism, a survival-of-the-fittest struggle where most just about kept their heads above water only to eventually succumb to exhaustion, but where someone occasionally emerged victorious. As such they also allowed for a reflection on the American dream and the idea that if you could just keep dancing long enough you could make it to the big time.

In many ways pedestrianism and marathon dancing mark the heyday of endurance sport, especially in terms of popular interest. Since baseball (and then basketball, football, Formula One and others) took over, endurance sport has never quite captured the popular imagination in the same way. Yet interest in ultra-distance challenges does seem to have surged recently and it is tempting to ask what it is about this particular moment that makes this the case. It also seems as if, with hindsight, we can say that a fascination with extreme endurance challenges tends to occur at moments of profound change, which are often characterised by tension and confusion.

Some of the earliest organised running events that took place in the Lake District, for example, were 'manhunt' games, organised by wealthy urban elites, including a number of Cambridge academics. George Trevelyan, who would become Regius Professor of History at Cambridge, described being chased across the fells in 1898 by the writer Geoffrey Winthrop Young as 'the most exciting five minutes I have ever had in my life, as we both went as hard as we possibly could over the chaos of wet rocks.' Whilst many have interpreted these games as a rejection of modernity, or the urban, the historian Jonathan Westaway argues that they were a way for powerful men to grapple with the idea of the end of the British Empire. Turning to the mountains was a way of refocusing scale, a way of gaining perspective not only in terms of space, but also time. The mountains were a reminder of geological time, of that which would endure. By switching roles from hunter to hunted, and struggling over the kind of rugged terrain on which many colonial wars were fought, these games were a kind of 'ritual of our own extinction'.

If the pedestrian period was characterised by anxieties about creeping mechanisation and the replacement of humans with machines, marathon dancing is a metaphor for Depression-era struggle, and manhunt games provided a rehearsal for the end of Empire, what kind of anxieties in the contemporary moment might be pushing people to find their own limits? This is not an easy question to answer, not least because so often it seems that these feats of endurance are at once a reflection of, and a reaction against, broader trends in society.

They are also, it seems, often characterised by a series of tensions or ambivalences – between work and play, between the individual and the collective, between freedom and constraint, and between 'authenticity' and the embrace of technology. On the one hand they are often about stripping back life to something more simple and profound, a return to what makes us fundamentally human, but on the other they are animated by our experiences of modern life and relate to a very modern kind of subject – an individual who wants to be in control of themselves, who wants to achieve within a system that ranks them against their peers.

As things like ultra-running and mountain biking grow in popularity, they gradually move from being counter-cultural to becoming aligned with the dominant culture of competition, ranking and rationalisation. As William Finnegan puts it in his surfing memoir, *Barbarian Days*, surfing 'was not a "sport". It was a "path". And the more you poured into it, the more you got from it.' Surfing, or at least one version of it, has very clearly moved into the mainstream, recently gaining the status of Olympic sport. In a sense these more counter-cultural or 'lifestyle' activities move from 'ritual to record', a trajectory that sports, the historian Allen Guttman has argued, also broadly follow. Gradually, the more ritualistic forms of meaning-making are replaced by institutionalisation, categorisation and especially comparison between countries and time periods. We come, in short, to worship the record.

This kind of shift away from seeing an activity like trail running as a 'path' to seeing it as a 'sport' is one that can clearly be identified by looking at the prestigious event, the Ultra-Trail du Mont-Blanc (UTMB). In 2023, it marked its 20-year anniversary on X by actively celebrating the shift away from a haphazard, do-it-yourself attitude: 'From soft chocolate with sandwich bread and sodas, to lactate blood tests and advanced energetic food, almost 20 years of UTMB.' Part of what I want to explore over the following chapters is what we might lose by embracing mid-race lactate tests and abandoning less calculated approaches to these kind of challenges. What of the ritual might we want to try to hold on to? To begin thinking about this question, and the broader question of what it is that makes us voluntarily do exhausting things, I travelled to the Sierra Madre to revisit the subject of the best-selling book on running, *Born to Run*.

2

RARÁMURI, MEXICO

'When the deer raises his tail, we're running'

– Rarámuri saying

I wake at 5.15 a.m. to the sound of the kettle clanking on the top of the wood-burning stove and emerge bleary-eyed to find Silvino stirring a dessert spoonful of sugar into a mug of Nescafé. Around the kettle, four fresh tortillas are starting to brown and last night's frijoles are bubbling gently next to them. I'd told Silvino that I don't normally eat before a morning run, but he'd shaken his head. 'It'll take a couple of hours to get to the bottom of the canyon,' he said. 'You don't want to be hungry when you turn round and look back up.' I conceded that he had a point.

We fill the tortillas with frijoles and eat slowly as the faintest hint of light begins to reveal the distant peaks of the 'Sierra Tarahumara'. As the cliffs become visible they take on a bluish tinge and I am relieved to feel that, whilst it is not exactly cool, the night has taken the edge off the oppressive heat. I hadn't realised when I'd booked my flights to Mexico, but I am here at the hottest time of year. When I arrived I told Silvino I wanted to see a 'real' Rarámuri trail and he grinned. 'In that case,' he said, 'I'll take you into the inferno.' We take enough water with us to get to the bottom of the canyon, where we can refill in a hamlet called Chapateri, and walk out into the semi-darkness.

Silvino's place is right at the edge of the village of Huisuchi, with only a few metres of dirt road to cover before we reach a rocky outcrop shaded with trees. Mickey, who has accompanied me on the trip, is up already, sipping coffee outside. '*No matalo!*' he says cheerfully as we walk out. 'Don't kill him!' After walking for a few minutes, Silvino asks, '*Quieres trottar un pocito?*' 'Do you want to jog for a bit?' I do and when we set off it is at what is best described as a trot. Silvino pecks his way across the ground in short steps, with very little wasted motion in his upper body. I try to mimic him and to 'follow his feet' as I was taught during my time running in Ethiopia, taking advantage of his far greater knowledge of the trail. He is wearing a pair of trail running shoes (referred to in Spanish as *tennis* for tennis shoes) rather than the traditional *huaraches*, having asked me the night before if I minded and seeming seemed quite relieved when I didn't.

Given the emphasis placed on footwear (or lack of it) in *Born to Run*, Chris McDougall's bestseller about the Rarámuri and 'the greatest race the world has never seen', it is not surprising that Silvino expected me to be interested in this as well. The trail running shoes were much more comfortable, though, and didn't come with the many potential issues of *huaraches,* which are made by cutting a piece of car tyre to the shape of the foot and then fastening it to the ankle with string. *Huaraches* are light and help you to feel the trail, but they also present a whole load of potential problems that running shoes do not – stones between the tyre and the feet, for example, or having to stop to retie or replace the snapped string that holds them in place. A particular issue is if they get wet, as they frequently do in crossing rivers in the *barrancas* or gorges – imagine trying to run fast with a piece of wet tyre flapping around underneath your foot.

There is a very clear tendency to focus on footwear and 'footstrike' – how your foot engages with the ground as you are running – in both popular and academic studies of runners in places like Kenya and Mexico. Often this is motivated by a desire by the author (usually white, male, injury-prone) to 'fix' their own problems with their running. Books are therefore written in which huge chunks are devoted to speculation about the benefits of more 'barefoot' and/or 'natural' approaches to running, which ironically tend to have the effect of launching huge new markets for innovatively 'simple' running footwear. For example, 'Barefoot Ted', who in *Born to Run* is described learning how to make *huaraches* from Manuel Luna, subsequently set up Luna Sandals, a company with revenues of over two million dollars in 2021.

Silvino agrees about the benefits of *huaraches*. They're light, and they allow you to 'feel' the trail well. But for a long run he would almost always opt for trail running shoes if he could, for the same reason I would – you don't want to 'feel' the trail too closely in a 100-mile race, you want to try to minimise the impact on your legs. Given his ambivalence towards *huaraches*, Silvino is amused by the global interest in barefoot running.

Part of the reason I'd wanted Silvino to show me a trail like the one we're on is because of his reaction to the questions I ask him about the race described in *Born to Run*. 'The problem with that race is that it was so short,' he says. He makes a distinction between races that require runners to be *legero* (light) and those that require *resistencia* (endurance). The Rarámuri, for the most part, excel at anything requiring *resistencia*. The longer the race and the more extreme the trail, the better. The race organised by Caballo Blanco (an enigmatic American runner who lived in Mexico and whose real name was Micah True), in the book was 50 miles, like a short road race by Rarámuri standards, run for the most part on the kind of roads we had driven up to Huisuchi on. It also had a defined finish line, which makes things somewhat easier. If the race described so evocatively by McDougall was a 'short road race', I was looking forward to hearing Silvino's stories about his more extensive races later on.

For the first part of the run we follow a faint dusty trail gradually downhill between big slabs of rock, and the netleaf oak and Apache pine trees overhead make it quite difficult to navigate in the semi-darkness. It gradually gets lighter as the trees thin and the sun gradually rises, and then we suddenly emerge from the trees and the world opens up in a way that is initially disorientating. It is as though the landscape has been rendered in a perspective beyond that normally comprehended by the human eye – like one of Andreas Gursky's large format photographs, only of innumerable sheer cliffs rather than tower blocks. There seem to be too many levels to the cliffs, slabs of rock and snaking trails, which make unlikely diagonals across the slopes at angles that look like they were conceived by Dutch graphic artist, MC Escher.

We pause to take it in. 'Look, there goes someone in the valley,' Silvino says, pointing downwards. It takes me a long time to find the figure, a tiny white speck moving uphill along a barely visible trail, and I realise that this is because I'd been looking for a figure several times larger. It is a very long way down. If our ability to run long distances corresponds to our ability to see them, then the Rarámuri's ability to cover extreme distances on foot suddenly begins to make a bit more sense. I start musing about this – the same is true in the Ethiopian highlands or on the edge of the Rift Valley where many top Kenyan runners train – but it is not long before the trail gets so technical that I can't concentrate on anything else.

In some sections the rocks are so big and the trail so steep that I have to lower myself down with my hands. In the less steep sections a fine white dust has pooled, with a layer of dry leaves on top which is incredibly difficult to get a purchase on. As my quads get increasingly beaten up by the downhill running I find it harder to follow Silvino's lead, until he seems to be perpetually waiting for me at the next rocky outcrop, gazing out across the canyon. Sound operates differently here, too. It seems like you can hear the tiniest sound from a mile away – a dry leaf crunching or a whip-poor-will's distinctive call – yet someone can appear around the corner of the trail completely unexpectedly.

Given how steep and unforgiving the trail is, this happens surprisingly often and gives me a welcome opportunity to rest whilst Silvino chats in *rarámuri*. The men wear brightly coloured tunics, often in orange or red, and white skirts that look like they've been starched. The people we meet are not running, but they're covering the trail fast wearing *huaraches*. All are walking for several hours, either to visit friends and relatives, or to buy or sell something, or some combination of the two. This is very clearly not conceived of as training, but it also wouldn't stand you in bad stead if you were preparing for a mountainous 100-mile race.

Silvino is clearly a bit concerned about my ability to cope on this kind of trail and with the heat, which is set to rise to 38 °C by midday. Every now and then he points down in the direction of Chapateri and says, 'Are you sure you want to keep going down?' I'm not really, but the whole point of this exercise is to put myself out of my comfort zone. 'Of course!' I say. I didn't bring a running backpack with me, so I'm carrying a bottle of water and can feel it going from cool to lukewarm in my sweaty palm. 'I used to carry lumber down these trails to sell. Sometimes 30 or 40kg at a time,' Silvino tells me. He mimes carrying logs on his back.

'You had to run the downhill sections because it's actually easier than walking,' he goes on. 'It shifts the weight around and you're less likely to fall.' I can kind of see what he means. It's so steep in a lot of places it would be impossible not to stumble into a jog with that much weight on your back. The lightweight running rucksack (with a few emergency tortillas and some water) he is carrying today must feel like nothing in comparison. I try to mimic the dancing steps he takes on the trail and the way he goes with any shifting in the scree under his feet, using the momentum to his advantage rather than fighting it. I've not run a continuous descent this long before and I notice that my quads are shaking.

Eventually we reach flatter ground and approach a couple of farmsteads in the valley. 'We can have tea with my brother,' Silvino says. As important as running is to the Rarámuri, they don't do anything that would resemble specific running training. It is already clear from spending a couple of days with Silvino that he has neither the time nor the inclination to run unless he is racing. It wouldn't make sense to him to spend time running that could be spent doing something more productive, like chopping wood, walking to a communal work project or driving neighbours to pick apples in Cuauhtémoc six hours away (which is what he is planning to do the day after we leave). I'm quite pleased that 'showing the anthropologist some trails' wasn't seen as a good enough reason to run for half a day and that this is also a good opportunity for him to visit his brother Silverio, who, like most of

Silvino's family, was a runner in his youth and had a reputation as one of the strongest *rarájipari* runners.

I am also glad that we are visiting Silverio because I can sit down and drink the cup of laurel leaf tea his wife hands me. Silverio is much older that Silvino, who can only just remember the races his brother ran in. He also has only a few teeth left and tells us about a race in rapid *rarámuri*, which Silvino translates into Spanish. 'The most memorable *rarájipari* I took part in was in Urique,' he says. The head of one of the two teams came up the valley to Huisuchi specifically to recruit him, because he heard he was such a strong runner – the way Silverio describes it, with a grin, is that he was 'kidnapped'. Silvino explains that this was quite an unusual *rarájipari* in that the teams were small – six runners on each – and it was only the strongest runners who were invited to take part.

'So he was kind of like a ringer in the all-star game?' I ask Silvino in English, who shrugs. *Rarájipari* involves huge amounts of running, but it is rarely described as a 'race'. It is a 'game' or is described as *la correra de bola* – running with the ball. It consists of two teams competing over a course that is usually a loop of between 5 and 6km. The 'short' version of the game can start at dawn and end at sunset, but often the number of laps stated at the start (30, in many examples I was given) make it effectively a last man standing event. Runners must 'throw' the wooden ball using their foot and a long wooden stick, meaning that *rarájipari* more closely resembles an epic game of croquet than extreme long-distance football.

'We ran something like 30 laps,' Silverio recalls, 'and at the end it was just me and one *campañero* left on our team.' I quickly do the maths and realise that this equates to 180km even without any detours to fetch the ball. He was able to keep going because, in spite of the fact that his official team had dwindled to two, he was surrounded by supporters from Urique, who ran alongside them (sometimes covering well over a marathon themselves), and surrounded them with chants and encouragement. 'When we realised we had won we both collapsed and had to be taken to the clinic,' he says. He ran 'a bit' after this race, but he was never the same again, he says, gesturing to his knee. The race was the definition of an 'all-in' approach to competition. Silverio didn't have much money to wager on the outcome of the race, so came away with 'only' 80 pesos, but Silvino recalls how far this money went the best part of 40 years ago. 'My memory of it was of him staggering back home with huge amounts of stuff,' Silvino says. It was the equivalent of him going away to work for over a month.

'I didn't just run *rarájipari*, you know,' Silverio says as we are getting up to leave and get back on the trail. 'I ran down deer as well.' I have a lot of questions – about this, about the betting that accompanies *rarájipari*, about the significance of the game itself, about how *on earth* anyone can run 180km without training, but we've got a canyon to escape from, so I resolve to save them for later. A local musician has offered to perform some of the songs that accompany *rarájipari* a few days later and Silverio promises to walk up to Huisuchi for this. 'It's best to tell running stories over tequila anyway,' he muses.

'Will we walk back or run?' I ask Silvino as we inspect the cliffs above us. The downside of our stop at Silverio's is that most of the shade in the canyon is now gone and the temperature must be in the mid-30s. '*Como lo siento*' is his response – 'As I feel.' We proceed, then, in a combination of running and fast walking, and I try to pick up the rhythm Silvino is making between the two. For the most part we run, trying to be as *legero* as possible, and maintaining this momentum helps us not to slip back down the slope. The sweat stings my eyes, and I have to stop every now and then to sip water, which is now about the temperature of a cup of tea that's been left to cool for five minutes.

As we get closer to the top I carefully round a corner on the trail that is no more than a foot wide, with a scree slope dropping away sharply to my left, and will my legs to keep moving up the incline. Silvino is waiting for me on a huge slab of rock. '*Muy duro*', ('Very hard'), he says, with a big smile on his face. I admire his ability to embody the Nietzschean ideal of embracing suffering so cheerfully, and try to channel this enthusiasm in spite of the heat and the altitude. As I struggle up the slope I'm once more reminded that my life as an anthropologist has consisted, much of the time, of making myself feel inadequate at something that is both one of my favourite things and probably the thing I do the best.

I'm quite relieved to see that Silvino does seem to be tired as well, and as we near the top of the canyon we turn back to look at where we've come from. 'How far do you think we've run?' I ask him. '*Es poco pero es muy pesado,*' is his response. 'Only a little, but it's very heavy work.' He thinks we've covered about 15 miles, but all of it up and down an incredibly steep slope. This is a trip that Silvino makes relatively regularly though, and often whilst carrying a load of corn or wood for his brother. He has owned a jeep for quite a few years now, but it is of absolutely no use to him on this terrain – the environment dictates that if he wants to see his brother he must walk, and if he wants to get there and back quickly he must run.

*   *   *

I travelled up to Huisuchi a few days earlier with Mickey Mahaffey, an American who has lived in the region for 20 years and has accompanied other researchers on trips into the canyons. Mickey is a fascinating person to spend time with, an itinerant philosopher with his own theories about long-distance walking. Diagnosed with arthritis in North Carolina decades ago and told that his joints might benefit from a more humid climate, he put a tarp and a change of clothes in a bag and set off to walk to Honduras. He has walked thousands of miles through the *barrancas* in all weather, sleeping outside most of the time, and he has easily enough stories to while away the hours in Chihuahua and Creel on our way to Huisuchi. He tells me about a particularly bad snowstorm in the canyons. In a break in the whiteout he spotted a hut and knocked on the door, looking for shelter. An old lady opened it. She took one look at the wide-eyed, white-bearded gringo and then, 'She just ignored me,' he says, laughing. 'She just fixed her eyes in the middle distance and straight up decided I didn't exist.' He headed back out into the snow.

He lives outside a lot when he's in North Carolina, too, and has long been something of an activist. He set up a free lunch for the local homeless at one point, only to have it shut down by a policeman. He was arrested for pointing out the hypocrisy of the policeman's 'WWJD' tattoo ('probably not this, asshole'), and had a column in the progressive Ashville daily newspaper for years. As a young man he had wanted to be a preacher, but eventually grew out of that in favour of a set of beliefs collected on the move in the Blue Ridge and Smoky Mountains. As we sit in *La Antigua Paz,* the oldest bar in Chihuahua, drinking *sotol* ('artisanal' tequila made by the Rarámuri) and beers, he tells me a story that has added to my apprehensions about the trip.

He tells it as though it's one of the funniest things that's ever happened to him. 'I had my third heart attack last time I was in Huisuchi,' he begins, 'so it's going to be a bit weird to be back.' He was heading to Arnulfo's house from Silvino's and had a heart attack halfway there before stumbling the rest of the way. Arnulfo won the race organised by Caballo Blanco (now the annual Ultra Marathon Caballo Blanco) in Urique that is described in such vivid detail in *Born to Run*. His house is in Munerici, a few miles from Huisuchi, and it is a long way from the dirt roads we would drive on. 'They put me in a wheelbarrow,' he says, 'and one of the women in the village attached an umbrella to it to keep the sun off me. Then they rolled me down bumpy trails for an hour before we could get in a truck and head to the medical centre another three hours away.' He takes a swig of beer.

'Shit,' I say. This often turns out to be the most appropriate response to his stories. 'When I saw the cardiologist back in North Carolina,' Mickey continues, 'he said, "I don't know why you're still alive," but he thinks all the shaking around on the trails might have kept the blood moving somehow...' Arnulfo now refers to the wheelbarrow as '*la ambulancia Rarámuri*'. He made Mickey a special pair of *huaraches* from the front tyre. The dirt roads we use to get up to Huisuchi were built primarily in order to allow the *narcotraficantes* to get drugs out of the canyons, but Mickey assures me that there is no danger from them. 'Everyone knows Silvino,' he says, so even if they stop us it will be fine. I'm now significantly more worried about Mickey's heart than I am about *narcos* or scorpions, but I am hoping that Silvino's truck is in good shape. 'There are places on that road where if you break down it's a three-day walk to get the parts to fix the truck,' Mickey notes.

The following morning we take a bus to Creel, where Silvino picks us up in his jeep, greeting Mickey like a long-lost friend. After a delicious lunch of *pozole* – a spicy meat stew with puffed corn – we set off for Huisuchi. As they catch up in Spanish, I try to re-read *Born to Run* in the back, until the bouncing of the jeep and the swirling dust make this impossible. There is so much dust rising from the road that it looks as though the trees and rocks have had a light coating of beige snow, and yet we don't see another vehicle for three hours. In McDougall's account, the canyons are 'wild and impenetrable', and populated by 'man-eating jaguars'. He writes that in order for the American participants to get to the start line of the race in Urique, 'They'd have to slip past bandits, hike through the badlands, keep an eagle eye on every sip of water and every bite of food. If they got hurt, they were dead.' It is safe to say that had I taken this literally I would have got straight back on the plane to London.

McDougall's account of the Ultra Marathon Caballo Blanco in Urique, which brings together some of the best ultra-runners in America with the best Rarámuri runners, is vivid and arresting. The first time I read it I devoured it in a couple of days. The book as a whole makes a case for endurance running defining our humanity and has inspired thousands upon thousands of runners, yet it contains surprisingly little about the Rarámuri themselves. There are entire chapters on American ultra-runners Scott Jurek and Ann Trason, for example, and we learn a lot about their motivations and what drives them. Jurek (who finished second in the race described in the book) is mentioned 204 times, whilst Silvino (the Rarámuri runner who was just behind him in third) is only mentioned 33 times. Although McDougall does make an attempt to interview Arnulfo, he didn't want to talk to an outsider. From this, it seems to me that McDougall assumed that it was not possible to talk to any of the Rarámuri runners at any length. However, of the many Rarámuri runners I interviewed, Arnulfo was the only one who *didn't* want to talk about running.

In most accounts of the Rarámuri they function as an undifferentiated type, representatives of what McDougall calls 'a near-mythical tribe of Stone Age superathletes'. This is a view that seems to be shared by many who become fascinated with Rarámuri athleticism. Of Joe Vigil, the American coach, McDougall writes that he believed that if he could understand American runner Ann Trason, he'd 'grasp what one amazing person could do'. However, if he could understand the Rarámuri, he'd 'know what everyone could do'. Similarly, if Scott Jurek could win the race in Urique, he writes, he wouldn't be beating Arnulfo and Silvino, he'd be demonstrating that he was 'the best of all time'.

These kinds of representations risk reinforcing outdated ideas about differences between the so-called 'savage' and the supposedly 'civilised'. In the anthropologist Carl Lumholtz's 19th-century account, this kind of characterisation is more apparent. The Rarámuri, he writes, 'certainly do not feel pain in the same degree that we do,' adding that he learnt this from collecting their hair. This is extended to what he says about Rarámuri running – they need not train, he writes, because running 'comes to them as naturally as swimming to a duck,' meaning they can 'easily run 170 miles without stopping.' Lumholtz writes extremely well elsewhere about the spiritual significance of Rarámuri running, but such writing about 'natural' physiological ability tends to play down the far more interesting meanings that are attached to the practice.

In this view, the Rarámuri represent humanity as a whole in an imagined pristine and physically superior state. This is why it rarely occurs to people to write about individual Rarámuri runners – because they are all supposedly 'running people'. Harvard anthropologist Dan Lieberman, who has himself spent a lot of time with the Rarámuri over the last 20 years, refers to this as the 'fallacy of the athletic savage'. That is to say, the idea that we should look to superior genetics to 'explain' the ability of runners from particular places, whether that be the highlands of Ethiopia and Kenya or the mountains of Mexico or Nepal, has the effect of reducing complex and often beautiful explanations to the search for one magic allele or genetic mutation.

There are others who assume there must be some other 'secret' to Rarámuri running prowess. As we bump along the track, Mickey tells me that he was approached by a Japanese film crew who wanted to make a documentary, because they had heard that the Rarámuri are so good because they run with rocks in their mouths. He had to politely tell them that no, he didn't think that was the case. A few weeks later they got back in touch and said they had heard that the Rarámuri used special breathing techniques. Mickey recalls calling Silvino to ask, 'Y'all do any special kind of breathing when you run?' Silvino had laughed and said, 'No, we just breathe.'

The idea of a 'running people' is compelling, of course. For those of us who like to cover long distances for fun, it is comforting to think that we are answering a call from our collective past and more fully inhabiting our human nature. Perhaps we are to some extent, but in focusing on things like footwear and 'stone-age' lifestyles we are missing a big part of this picture. In order to capture more of this, it is vital to ask *why* Rarámuri people run; to try to articulate the social significance of running in Rarámuri culture; and to explain how it fits into the rest of their lives.

* * *

After our run into the canyon, Silvino, Mickey and I spend most of the next few days in Huisuchi and Sorachique talking to as many people as we can about running in a mix of Spanish and *rarámuri*. One thing that seems clear is that there are far fewer *rarájipari* now than there were in the past. This is put down to a number of different factors. Firstly, there is an increasing need to make money, for instance by working to harvest apples in places like Cuauhtémoc. When most people were subsistence farmers there were quiet periods of the year when *rarájipari* were organised 'just for something to do', as Silvino puts it. Given that it often takes between a week and two weeks to recover from a *rarájipari*, it is harder to find the time (and energy) to hold them now. In fact, many of the races that do take place are facilitated by organisations with a remit to preserve traditional culture.

We speak to a woman named Canta La Luna, who is in her seventies and was committed to continuing to organise *rarájipari* and the women's equivalent, *ariwete* races, for many years. Rather than kicking or 'flicking' a ball, *ariwete* is arguably a lot more skilful and involves teams rolling a hoop with a stick over rough ground, with races often lasting a day or a day and a half. Preparations for a big race, including the food and *tesquino*, an alcoholic drink made from fermented corn, could take weeks, whilst collecting the bets became almost a full-time job.

'Why was it important to you to keep the races going?' I ask her. 'We were the ones staying put on this land whilst everyone else was going here and there,' she says, gesturing around her. 'So we wanted to stay here and do it right.' I ask her what 'doing it right' meant to her. 'Onoruame likes it when the betting is really big and the music is clean, and the running goes on for a long time,' she says. Onoruame, or Father Sun, is the traditional God of the Rarámuri. 'The music is especially important, because the emotion of running is very important to Onoruame.' Playing instruments and dancing traditional dances for hours and often days on end can be almost as exhausting as the running.

Another factor in the decrease in *rarájipari* and *ariwete* – which was also a worry for those keen to preserve Ethiopian distance running dominance – has been the introduction of the cell phone. When Silvino talks about his childhood, the main thing he recalls is running *rarájipari* at every opportunity – in breaks from school, at lunchtime, after school until it was too dark to see the ball. Running was the principal form of entertainment in a way that for most people it is not any more. The proliferation of *marathones*, partly a result of the interest generated by the race organised by Caballo Blanco in Urique, is also a factor, although in most cases these were seen as less lucrative than *rarájipari*. Many ultras have started to offer financial incentives further down the field, though, with food tokens given out to Rarámuri runners for completing each 20km of an ultra-race, for example.

In this sense running *marathones* remains implicated in what Silvino says is one of his main motivations for running – or for doing anything particularly arduous – *necesidad*. Necessity. He uses the same word to describe how he was able to keep going towards the end of a *rarájipari*. If you've staked enough to win the equivalent of several months' earnings, that's likely to keep you going. But there is a far larger significance to *rarájipari* that is absent from *marathones* and which requires interviewing musicians as well as runners to understand.

*　*　*

Herculeo arrives with his son and his violin in the early evening, and Silvino quickly disappears inside to grab a bottle of *sotol*.

'You can't play without a drink,' he reasons. As a small group of people gather in the yard, Mickey produces a packet of Faros cigarettes and passes them round. By the time the sun goes down and we're settling into the pleasant buzz of two or three tequilas, I ask Silvino to tell me about his most memorable *rarájipari*. 'OK,' he says, clapping his hands together. 'I'll tell you about a race where I beat Arnulfo and ran most of the way alone.' Silverio is nodding. 'This one is pretty legendary around here,' he says, but he seems happy to hear it again.

'When I race Arnulfo the betting is usually pretty big,' he starts. 'We've been rivals since long before that race in *Born to Run*. We grew up racing each other at every break in the school day and we're always on opposing teams when we play *rarájipari*.' High stakes make it more likely that the race will go on and on, and this is very clearly a factor in motivating people to run. 'The thing with *rarájipari*,' he says, 'is that it's much easier to lose. If the stakes are low it's easy to just stop and settle for some soda and crackers.' This means that, contrary to what you might expect, people will sometimes bet *more* when they think they're going to lose, in order to put pressure on themselves to run well.

Even after his many years of playing *rarájipari* Silvino is still a little unsure of what it all means. He admits to being curious about why anybody runs long distances. 'It is a kind of suffering,' he says, sipping his *sotol*. 'We kick the ball and kick rocks at the same time. We tear up our feet and toenails. Why do we keep running?' We laugh. '*Muy curioso*,' he adds. 'When we feel like we're going to lose we bet more, and when we feel like we're going to win we bet less, because it makes us nervous.' *Muy curioso* indeed.

It is important not to understate the importance of the betting that accompanies *rarájipari*. In Lumholtz' account, in fact, the interest in *rarájipari* 'centres almost entirely in the betting that goes with it; in fact, it is only another way of gambling.' I wouldn't go quite this far – there is certainly less romance in writing about 'the gambling people' than there is in painting a portrait of 'the running people' – but it does seem like the intrigue and the chance to win life-changing amounts of money at the expense of your neighbours account for a large amount of the interest in *rarájipari*. Very often when I asked people to recount the most exciting race they had been involved in, they started with an account of what they had won. 'I won a horse once,' was how one old man began his tale.

The quantities of money and goods bet on *rarájipari* don't make a great deal of rational sense when you consider that people are often living pretty close to a subsistence lifestyle. This is similar in some respects to the situation described in one of the most well-known anthropology articles ever written, Clifford Geertz's 'Deep Play: Notes on the Balinese Cockfight'. The article is best known for introducing and defending the use of 'thick description' in anthropology, opening with a vivid account of a police raid on a cockfight in Bali that Geertz and his wife were attending. Whilst many anthropologists have looked at sport as a trivial matter that is separate from more significant elements of 'culture' like religion or the way the economy is organised, Geertz notes that the Balinese cockfight is central to the way Balinese people understand themselves. The cockfight is 'a story they tell themselves about themselves,' he writes.

Much like *rarájipari*, the size of the central bet made in cockfighting 'makes the game' as Geertz puts it, or signals its 'depth' to use the utilitarian philosopher Jeremy Bentham's term. 'Deep play,' according to Bentham's *Theory of Legislation*, published in 1802, means play in which the stakes are so high that from a utilitarian point of view it is irrational to engage in it. Bentham gives the example of someone with a fortune of £1000 making an evenly matched bet of £500. In this scenario the costs of losing far outweigh the benefits of winning, so making such bets represents, in Bentham's view, the behaviour of 'addicts and fools'.

Bentham thinks that, if possible, such bets should be made illegal, but as Geertz explains, in Bali people do not see the money attached to the cockfight in the same utilitarian way. The money is 'less a measure of utility' and more 'a symbol of moral import'. He goes on to write that in the bets attached to the cockfight there is 'much more at stake than material gain: namely, esteem, honour, dignity, respect – in a word, though in Bali a profoundly freighted word, status.' In short, to quote the austere philosopher Jessie J, 'It's not about the money.'

It is because people stand to lose (or gain) so much from the cockfight that it has such a draw in terms of status. Rather than representing irrationality as it would to Bentham, this serves to increase the meaningfulness of it all. The more money is involved, the more the cockfight serves to represent the Balinese status hierarchy more broadly. It becomes a 'status bloodbath', as he puts it. The cockfight therefore becomes a kind of proxy battle between groups of friends and neighbours, a way of 'playing with fire without getting burnt.' In spite of the intense drama of the cockfight, the agony and ecstasy it provokes, Geertz writes that 'nothing really changes.' In this sense, attending a cockfight is a bit like watching a Shakespeare play: it allows people to reflect on their own society in a detached and safe way.

The problem with this symbolic interpretation of the cockfight is that it misses a very crucial point: Balinese cockfights had very real and genuinely horrific consequences for some kinds of people. Historically, Balinese kings would host cockfights as a way of enticing the poorest into losing everything, whereupon they would be sold into slavery along with their children. With *rarájipari*, it seems that the runners are quite conscious of using the betting as a way of increasing the meaningfulness and excitement of the races, but it is very clear that this is not merely of symbolic value: there are races that you can genuinely scarcely afford to lose, where motivation springs from necessity.

It should also be clear that unlike the cockfight, which is a 'proxy' battle, in *rarájipari* people really race against each other, so the competition is far more direct. Arnulfo and Silvino's rivalry goes beyond running, encompassing the houses they have been able to build and the people they are able to support through their success. Running, then, is deeply embedded in determining people's success in life and the respect they receive from their community. The process of assembling the teams of runners, and discussions about how to place bets and how much to risk, create intrigue and excitement for weeks leading up to a big race, drawing the whole community into the event in a way that would be difficult without the betting element.

The night before the race, the runners from each team gather to prepare themselves. Each team has a shaman, who blesses the bets the runners will place on themselves and who conducts rituals to prepare them to compete. This magical element is extremely important – it is common for people to blame losing a *rarájipari* on the powerful magic of the opposing shaman. In a sense, then, there is a race within the race, as the shamans compete to bring their teams a victory. As an example, Silvino says that because human bones are thought to induce fatigue, these are sometimes dug up and hidden where the opposing team will need to pass. The runners' muscles are rubbed with stones and herbs to prepare them to run, and then they are led on a ceremonial circuit around a wooden cross, walking around it as many times as they will run laps in the race.

As we are talking, Silvino's friend Patricio arrives with a wicker basket and slowly ties what look like two dried-up snakeskins around his legs. In fact, these are made from reeds and seed pods, and are similar to the rattles runners wear in *rarájipari* to keep them awake and alert. Behind him the full moon has begun to appear on the horizon, vast and orange. Patricio is taking the role of *pascolero* this evening and will show us the dances (*pascol*) that accompany the pre-race ritual. Most of the songs Herculeo plays are named after animals and are called things like '*Chumari*' (deer) or '*Rowi*' (rabbit), and beautiful sound is intended to establish a connection between the runner and the spirit of the animals, helping them to run like a deer or a hare the following day. According to the anthropologist Daniel Noveck, many other Rarámuri songs refer to movement between two places – the descriptive 'I go down to the river below, to carry things back', for instance. Singing these songs as part of pre-race rituals – and during the races themselves – serves to remind runners of the importance of movement in Rarámuri life.

Patricio begins by walking a barefoot circle around the gravel yard in front of Herculeo, before he begins a shuffling, rhythmical dance, tracing circles and figures of eight in the dust. As Carl Lumholtz notes, this may, in fact, only loosely be referred to as dancing. 'In reality,' he writes, it is more 'a series of monotonous movements, a kind of rhythmical exercise.' The word for 'dancing' is *nolavoa*, which actually means 'work' and dancing is, as Lumholtz puts it, 'a very serious and ceremonious matter'. Like running, it is as much a matter of worship or incantation as it is a form of amusement. The movement is somehow not monotonous, and there is something compelling in the repetitive and trance-inducing rhythm as others join in with Patricio.

Silvino and Silverio offer a few explanations for this dancing style. The feet pattering on the ground are intended to keep negative forces down below, to literally stamp down any bad vibes. The figure of eight symbolises continuity and keeping the world going, much like *rarájipari* does. In a sense the ceremonial laps of the cross the night before the race also resemble what sports psychologists might call visualisation, allowing the runners to commit to the race ahead and imagine themselves (somehow) running 180km.

The dancing the night before the race only lasts around an hour, because the race the following morning begins at dawn, but other dances can go on for days. Both running and dancing are described to me variously as a way of giving thanks to God or as a way of asking for things like rain or a full harvest. Part of this is that there is a real respect for hard work and endurance – the longer they are able to go on, the higher the praise. At dances it is important to drink as much *tesquino* as possible, because it embodies the work that went into harvesting the corn and the grace of God.

'What is more important,' I ask, 'dancing or running?' They are '*mas o menos egual*' Silvino says – 'more or less the same'. They serve the same purpose of giving thanks to God, by putting on a performance of vigour and endurance. I reflect on how differently we think about the equivalent activities in the UK. Someone who runs 100km races at the weekends may be thought of as a little crazy, but they are also likely to be seen as doing something that is in a sense virtuous and requires self-sacrifice and discipline. In contrast, someone who spends their weekends at raves, drinking heavily and dancing all night is likely to be seen very differently.

The dance festivals that the Rarámuri hold feature a combination of the kinds of rhythmic dancing Patricio has demonstrated, and sprinting backwards and forwards. The biggest annual festival is held during Semana Santa, and features running and dancing for upwards of 30 hours at a time. Mickey attended these originally as an observer, but was recruited to dance as one of the *diablos* (devils) who 'mess with' the Christians in the dances. In the 17th century the Jesuits tried to convert the Rarámuri, attempting to ban betting and drinking *tesquino*, but this was bound to fail. The current mixture of existing traditions and Christian festivals was later instigated by the Franciscans.

'No-one who writes about the Rarámuri really mentions the dancing,' Mickey says, gesturing towards Patricio. 'A lot of the guys who were diablos with me had also run in *rarájipari* and *marathones*, and they said the dancing at Semana Santa was way harder than the Ultra Caballo Blanco…'

'Of course,' Silvino says. 'No comparison.'

'So is the idea to get into a state of exhaustion and trance?' I ask.

'With all that beer, and all that physical exertion, it puts you in a really unique state,' Mickey says.

'I mean I was drunk *as shit*, but at the same time I was very clearly present in myself and with our group. Real lucid, but drunk at the same time. It's hard to describe. So when they worship God they're serious about it. There's no dressing up pretty for an hour's sermon in a church, then go home and forget about it.'

I realise that we have strayed quite a long way from an account of Silvino's race, but stories of running and dancing are often intertwined. 'The main thing people remember about this particular race against Arnulfo,' Silvino continues, 'is that I ran on my own after the first three or four laps, whilst he had 10 or 11 runners.' This is not to say that Silvino ran alone. Whilst his official teammates had dropped out, leaving him the only one who could 'throw' the ball with his foot (so described because this is more a controlled flick, often guided with a stick as well as the foot, than a Roberto Carlos free kick), he was surrounded by supporters, who shouted '*Iweriga! Iweriga!*', which means both 'soul' and 'breath' in *rarámuri*. 'You should have seen my feet by the end of the day,' he says. 'The second and third toes were down to the bone from throwing the ball.'

As darkness fell, Silvino was handed a lit torch, made from resinous pine wood, and surrounded by friends and supporters who carried a combination of flaming wood and torches. 'There were so many people with me, even in the night,' he recalls. 'Children, old people, both men and women.' Describing a similar race a hundred or so years earlier, Lumholtz writes that, 'The scene [is] one of extreme picturesqueness, as these torch-bearers, demon-like, hurry through the forest.' Silvino had, improbably, started to move away from Arnulfo and his team. 'I'm very good at throwing the ball,' he says. 'I can just pick a spot on the trail and hit it. That saves you a lot of time searching in the bushes.' Every lap, his team of musicians, led by Herculeo, would run alongside him for as long as they could, playing the same energetic and uplifting songs we are hearing this evening, before falling dead silent when Arnulfo went past.

During the night it was the two teams of musicians that gave Silvino a sense of how the race was developing. Arnulfo's band began to sound very distant, meaning that the gap between them was growing. Silvino realised that his best chance of winning – and of winning in the most prestigious way possible – was to catch Arnulfo. If one team gets a full lap ahead of the other, the race is over and so, in the dark, he started hunting. 'I was obviously pretty tired at this point,' he says, 'but the more I started to gain on him the more alert and animated I started to feel. I was wearing bells which jingled more the faster I went, so I focused on keeping the music going and on moving towards the light of Arnulfo's party.'

Silvino had bet enough on the outcome of this race to win the equivalent of what he would make for six weeks of hard agricultural work in the fields. He ran in a mass of people who had also bet on him winning this race and whose shouts of encouragement grew louder the closer he got to Arnulfo. 'Some of those people must have run 10, even 15, laps with me,' he says – 60 to 100km. 'And more than anything, I *really* wanted to beat Arnulfo,' he adds. 'We've been desperate to beat each other since we were six years old.' As he began to close in, he entered a trance-like state. The jangling of the bells and the shouts of his *campañeros* combined with the extreme exertion to create a kind of sensory overload, whilst his vision narrowed to the light bobbing in the distance that represented Arnulfo's team.

'Once I knew I was within striking distance,' he says, 'I realised I would have to be decisive.' Just like hunting a deer, he might only have one chance to run Arnulfo down – if he spooked him too early he'd be gone and the chance of winning the race this way would be over. He left his supporters behind and began to run like a man possessed, flaming torch in his fist, *huaraches* kicking up the dry earth behind him. Arnulfo's team tried to respond, but it was all over. Not one to accept the humiliation of being lapped, once he could hear the bells at Silvino's ankles, Arnulfo abandoned the race.

'At that point I more or less collapsed,' Silvino says. 'I spent most of the next two weeks in bed,' he laughs. 'It was worth it, though. People still talk about that night.' Arnulfo and Silvino have become important figures locally, partly due to their prowess as *rarájipari* runners and partly due to the money and respect that came with competing well in *marathones* and featuring in *Born to Run*. There is a sense, though, that the political and economic power they hold pre-dates their appearance in McDougall's book. Silvino was head of the local *ejido*, or farmers' association, before this, in a position to make difficult decisions about planting and irrigation that would affect the whole community. The ability to lead a *rarájipari* team to victory clearly brings a respect that transcends its status as a game.

As he sits on the hood of his Chevrolet Suburban with a mug of tequila in his hand, listening to the music, in front of the house he largely built himself, Silvino cuts a contented figure this evening. Herculeo begins to play the upbeat and lilting 'Deer Song' and I can tell that Silvino has enjoyed recounting the race with Arnulfo. I ask Silverio to tell us what it was like to hunt deer on foot. Did he catch them? Silvino translates: '*A veces sí, a veces no.*' 'Sometimes yes, sometimes no.' 'Did they hunt them primarily for food or as a diversion?' I ask. 'It is always both,' Silverio says with a grin.

This is similar to how another old man I spoke to described a job he had in his youth, of running down escaped horses whilst carrying just a small flask of *pinole*. 'Well, someone had to do it,' he'd said. 'I needed the money, of course, but it was kind of fun at the same time.' It is the same in Silvino's descriptions of Rarámuri runners who carry drugs out of the canyons and into the USA for the *narcotrafficantes* – they do so out of necessity *and* out of a sense of adventure.

'There's a phrase in *rarámuri*,' Silverio adds with a grin: 'When the deer raises his tail, we're running.' It is extremely rare for people to hunt in this way now, because the introduction of the rifle has wiped out the majority of the deer in the region. When deer were more plentiful, however, Silverio used to hunt them on foot even when he had access to a rifle. The trick was to know the usual routes the deer took so well that you could run them into a trap or else to force them on to rocky terrain that would eventually damage their hooves.

'Isn't it easier to use a rifle?' I ask.

'Of course,' Silverio says. 'But if you use a rifle, Tata Dios doesn't eat.' God never blessed the rifle so, as Silvino explains, seeing deer hunted in this way is 'not something that God likes to see.'

'So what does God like to see?' I ask.

'Well, God is happiest when he sees people running, dancing and drinking *tesquino*.'

Tesquino is corn beer. I like the sound of this God.

The crucial thing to understand about running *rarájipari*, hunting deer on foot and dancing is that these are all forms of prayer or worship. This is something that is not often emphasised when anthropologists study persistence hunting. Often these accounts aim to measure the efficacy and efficiency of hunting in this way. They look at the various anatomical adaptations that have evolved in humans, such as short toes and elongated Achilles tendons, and physiological ones like the high density of sweat glands that allow us to keep cool on the move, and compare the probabilities of catching animals using different hunting techniques and how efficient a use of energy this is in cost-benefit terms.

What interrogating persistence hunting in terms of whether or not it is an efficient use of energy misses, however, is the fact that an excessive outpouring of energy may very well be the point of it, as opposed to an unwelcome side-effect. Much like in Geertz's analysis of seemingly over-exuberant cock fighting betting, to analyse these things in the terms of cost-benefit calculations or rational decisions about calorie expenditure is to apply an alien value system. For many of the people I talked to, completing a *rarájipari*, or making a successful persistence hunt, required accepting unpredictability and the necessity for sometimes extreme feats of endurance, so those activities represented the challenge of navigating the various challenges life tends to throw at you. Therefore, whether as a metaphor for successfully navigating life or as a means of giving praise for the things that sustain life, it makes sense that races, dances and persistence hunts are conducted on a pretty epic scale.

If running *rarájipari* is 'a story the Rarámuri tell themselves about themselves', to borrow Geertz's phrase, it is one of people who are strong, who persevere in spite of unpredictable circumstances, and who will fight until they are barely conscious for their village and their neighbours. Often when people write about running they emphasise things like simplicity – it is the 'purest' sport, stripped of artifice, it taps more deeply than other sports into our common human 'nature'. There has been a tendency to declare the Rarámuri 'the running people', showing us the purity of what was possible before our lifestyles became sedentary and our running became complicated with smart watches, Strava segments and £250 shoes.

Rather than uncovering a stripped back, 'natural' way of running in Mexico, in fact I found a form of running that is far more complex and meaningful than our own, and which very clearly reflects broader values of *resistencia* in Rarámuri culture. The modernisation of Rarámuri running, and the replacement of *rarájipari* with *marathones,* actually represents a gross simplification of the activity of running for the Rarámuri. The betting and intrigue are gone, along with the pre-race rituals and the music and the accompanying magic. 'Does Tata Dios like it when you run *marathones*?' I ask Silvino. 'I don't think so,' he says. 'It's like hunting deer with a rifle.' The only tracking most of us do now is of ourselves and we track an ever-increasing number of variables. It is to this that I now turn.

3

THE ART OF TRACKING

'I don't want a watch making that decision for me'
– *Charlie Spedding, former long-distance*
runner and Olympic medallist

In 1927 the political artist John Heartfield created a photo-montage cover for *Der Knuppel* magazine. Entitled 'A Spectre is Haunting Europe: Rationalisation on the March', it was intended as an explicitly anti-fascist image. In the picture, giant legs made of industrial chimneys stride purposefully from right to left. The figure's arms are made from pistons, and its torso from a time-card used to stamp in and out of work in a factory. The head of the figure is a stopwatch. The image – created almost a century ago – clearly articulates a set of concerns we still have today about automation and the replacement of human workers with robots. But what does this have to do with running?

At the time when Heartfield was creating art, many of the best runners in the world came from Finland and their success was often attributed in romantic terms to the 'qualities' of the Finnish landscape. As the German journalist Jack Schumacher put it, writing in the 1930s, 'Running is certainly in the blood of every Finn. When you see the clear, deep green forests, the wide-open luxuriant plains with their typical red peasant homes [...] and the never-ending light blue of the horizon with the lakes merging with the sky, one is overcome with an involuntary feeling of elation and because you don't have wings, you want to run.' It is interesting that we don't see arguments about the genetic advantage of Finnish runners anymore (we are more likely to hear that running is 'in the blood' of Kenyans or Ethiopians), but what is most striking about this description is its romance.

We get the word fartlek ('speed play') from neighbouring Sweden, which conjures up an intuitive and playful approach to training, and the idea of athletes taking to the forest 'because a particular dreamlike quality enticed them and pulled them into the spell of its mysteries' (Schumacher again) is compelling. It was against this backdrop of pristine forests and a running that was seen to spring from a desire to commune with nature that in the early 1920s Paavo Nurmi emerged blinking from the Industrial School of Helsinki, top of his class in mathematics. Keen to apply what he had learnt about maths and scientific management to his running, he became the first runner to carry a stopwatch with him on training runs and to aim to run at a carefully controlled pace.

Soon he became so used to this way of running that he began to carry the watch in races as well, provoking an outcry from many involved in athletics at the time. Popular cartoons depicted Nurmi variously as a stopwatch on legs, his body turned into a machine by the demands of the clock, and as a stiff-limbed robot lurching forward like a figure from an early Egyptian frieze, a chimney emerging from his head. The *National Biography of Finland* account of Nurmi describes him as 'like a machine which, chugging away in businesslike fashion, ground down his opponents.'

All of which is to say that current debates about self-tracking and the adoption of technologies intended to help endurance athletes to 'know themselves' better have a history that goes back almost a century. And yet we have seemingly become far less concerned about the effects of all of this, even as we become more able to track the minute variations in our heartbeats or scrutinise live readings of our glucose levels with an app. I have always been relatively sceptical even about using GPS watches and heart rate monitors, brought up as a runner as I was by a coach who was very much of the old school. Max ran with the great Brendan Foster and Charlie Spedding at Gateshead Harriers, and whilst they had some roughly measured training routes and wore running watches, they certainly weren't concerned with heart rate zones.

I am, however, curious to explore the benefits of measuring my training and recovery in a more granular way. Maybe these technologies could rescue a perennially injured runner from the temptation to train too hard or too soon, and help me to know when I am recovered and when I should back off in training a bit, concerns that are amplified by trying to balance continuing to do some running and cycling with working full-time and parenting small children.

I sit at the kitchen table and unpack some boxes. I have already been wearing a Whoop band on my wrist for a few months. It uses HRV, or heart rate variability, to create daily values for 'strain' on a scale of 1 to 21, 'recovery', measured as a percentage, and another percentage score for 'sleep performance'. I unpack a 'glucose sport biosensor' called the Libre Sense, which is made by a company called Abbott and was sent to me by another company called Supersapiens, who have developed an app to help visualise and translate the live glucose readings for use by athletes.

Wearing the Whoop band is basically like wearing a watch strap, but the glucose sensor is a little more complicated. I unpeel the covering to reveal a big chunk of plastic with a needle in the middle and watch the instruction video in the app. This tells me reassuringly that the needle will not actually stay in my arm, but will instead only be 'used to help insert the 5mm long, flexible hair-like filament under your skin', which doesn't sound creepy or invasive in the slightest. The sensor isn't actually painful to apply, however, and is soon secured on to my arm with the Ironman-branded sticker that came with it. According to the Supersapiens website I have now begun the 'journey of becoming supersapien'. An hour later I can see a live reading of my blood glucose level and I watch it rise after I eat a handful of biscuits.

As the feminist theorist Donna Haraway puts it, winning the Olympics in the cyborg era isn't just about running, cycling or climbing fast. It's about 'the interaction of machine, diet, training practices, clothing and equipment manufacture, visualisation and timekeeping'. A cyborg is a living being whose abilities have been enhanced by implants or mechanical body parts. When we imagine a cyborg we are far more likely to conjure up an image of RoboCop than someone running with a watch or their phone and headphones, but even these seemingly mundane technologies change our relationship with endurance sport.

For some thinkers, human potential is best achieved by escaping or repressing our animal origins and embracing technology to optimise our human capabilities. Here the aim of technology is to free the mind as far as possible from the constraints of the body. For others, we are already in the *posthuman* cyborg era; so intertwined with technology that our human nature is blurred beyond recognition; so enmeshed with new technologies that we are unable to think critically about our relationship with them.

The symbiotic relationship between humans and technology modifies human identity profoundly, marking a new era in human history.

Others argue that it is vitally important to think carefully about these technologies, because at some point bionic athletes' achievements will be primarily attributed to the creator of the technology rather than the athletes themselves. From my point of view this is actually the biggest issue with the way the two-hour marathon was reported on and marketed – the transcendent achievements of Eliud Kipchoge were in some cases overshadowed by those of shoe and apparel designers, as Mo Farah's were through the emphasis on zero-gravity treadmills and other innovations strongly associated with Nike.

Like many other tracking devices, Supersapiens promises to help people to 'become the best version of yourself', through harnessing a new level of insight into your body. This is the claim made by all the companies involved in self-tracking – that the data they generate will allow you to understand yourself better, and therefore to make better decisions about how to move and rest and eat. What does seem to be new with devices like Whoop and the Oura ring (another device that measures HRV, but through a ring rather than a wrist strap), though, is the attempt to make this kind of analysis a holistic one that encompasses all that we do, rather than just tracking and analysing specific activities, as we would with a device like a GPS watch.

The main way in which Whoop says it will help people understand themselves better is through a 'strain' score that takes into account not only exercise, but also the effects of a stressful meeting or the two hours you spent chasing your children around the park. Whilst all of these things clearly do influence our ability to 'perform', is seeking 'optimisation' in everything we do actually a good way to live? It might make sense for Whoop's CEO to maximise his sleep 'performance' by sleeping with an eye mask in a separate room to his wife and always going to bed at the same time, but do we all want to live like a CEO?

Finally, I open a small box from Forth Edge, a company that provides sports-specific blood tests in order to 'give you unparalleled insights into how your body works, races and recovers.' After some painful finger pricking I squeeze some blood into the vials and package everything up to send back for analysis. It occurs to me that the regular monitoring of blood values that companies like this encourage almost exactly mirrors that of the Athlete Biological Passport (ABP), the principal way in which World Athletics attempts to identify athletes who are doping. The difference, of course, is that this is a service amateur athletes pay a fairly significant amount of money for and that they have access to any insights that come from the data collected.

In a video advert that circulated online under #KnowYourself, Whoop makes the claim that 'you know the inside of everything except *you*.' This is a bold claim from a company that produces a device that can't tell the difference between digging a pond and mountain biking (my non-existent bike ride was apparently 'automatically detected' from 3.20 to 4.37 p.m. one afternoon as I sweated with a spade) and which routinely thinks I'm asleep when I'm sitting reading a book. For most people these kinds of estimates will be less important than the raw heart-rate data that they are based on, but you can understand why I might question the accuracy of that too.

For several months I wear the Whoop band on my left wrist and my Garmin watch on my right, and it is quite remarkable how different the data can be across the two devices. On one gravel bike ride in the summer of 2022, Whoop had my average heart rate at 136, whilst the reading from Garmin was 97. This was quite an extreme discrepancy, but it was common for the readings to be a difference of 20 beats per minute. Given the increasing tendency to base training for running and cycling on particular heart rate 'zones', this is quite a significant issue: theoretically you could follow a marathon training plan based on heart rate zones for months and never actually be in the correct zone.

I suppose these discrepancies could be explained by one of the devices being faulty. Luckily, though, I am able to talk to Kieran Alger, who spends a lot of his time wearing multiple devices in order to review them for companies and magazines, including, recently, as he ran a marathon a day along the length of the Danube river. Part of the reason for this is explicitly to make side-by-side comparisons, but often it's just because he only has a certain amount of time to write the reviews. 'If I had more arms I'd probably wear more watches,' he grins when I talk to him on Zoom.

The discrepancies he has seen between devices exists both between brands and between products from the same brand. You can wear two GPS watches at once and do exactly the same run and end up with different readings, because how they calculate distance will depend on which signals they pick up at the beginning of the run. Accuracy can often be affected by the time of day you run, too, because it depends on the relative position of satellites orbiting the earth at different times. The bigger differences, though, are when it comes to measuring heart rate.

'I've been on runs where I've been wearing a watch on each wrist,' says Kieran, 'and I've looked down and one watch is 20 beats higher than the other, then I've kept running for a bit and looked down again and they've switched places, but they're still 20 beats apart.' This is obviously an issue when it comes to monitoring your effort during a run if you are relying on an accurate heart rate reading. But now that most watches also use these readings to calibrate all kinds of other suggestions about how you train and how much you rest this becomes a bigger issue.

'Most of these devices will take the heart rate readings and other data and wrap them up into some kind of readiness score or assessment of stress,' he explains, 'so if it is incorrect you will also get very different recovery and stress readings.' When he ran the Danube, for instance, he wore the same watches throughout, and they gave quite different recovery estimates and suggestions each day. When it comes to tracking different stages of sleep (Whoop, for example, tells you how long you have spent awake, in 'light' sleep, in 'REM' sleep and in 'SWS' or 'deep' sleep), they are even less reliable. 'With sleep stages there are big discrepancies between the devices, but the inconsistencies are also inconsistent,' he says. 'If that makes sense?'

I'm starting to struggle to follow him, so I'm glad when he clarifies: 'One day one watch thinks I'm asleep when I'm watching TV. The next day it gets it right, but the other one doesn't,' he says. Kieran's interest in running started with the early wearable technologies – Nike's FuelBand and GPS devices that had to be strapped to the upper arm – and a lot of the appeal of running for him is in 'self-analytics and the data side of things'. He has access to more information about how the various wearable brands produce metrics like 'readiness' and 'recovery' scores. 'My personal relationship with technology,' he says, 'is that if I don't understand how or why it's generated the numbers, then I don't know whether to trust it or not.'

This is becoming more of a challenge, because, as he puts it, 'Some of the algorithms are getting very deep and entwined, and the sports science behind the numbers is difficult to penetrate.' For someone like Kieran, this presents a challenge, because as the companies involved become less willing to show their working and more prescriptive in the advice that they give, it becomes difficult to properly interrogate the numbers they produce and make informed decisions.

I am especially intrigued by the increasing use of HRV as a way of understanding our readiness to train or compete, because it is explicitly marketed as a way to capture all of life's other stressors, as well as whatever physical activity we are doing, and distil it into one numerical value. In simple terms, HRV is simply a measure of the variation in time between each heartbeat. If you are more stressed, or closer to fight-or-flight mode, the variation tends to be lower. If you're more relaxed, it tends to be higher, so Whoop can roughly calculate your level of stress and preparedness for exercise. In my experience, though, the Whoop recovery score, calculated as a percentage using HRV, often failed to map how I was actually feeling. It did, to be fair, get it right in an unusually extreme scenario – when I checked it after a four-hour sleep in a sleep pod in Dubai airport, after running 60km and drinking seven or eight beers the day before, it said I was 1% recovered. This felt about right, although it did make me wonder what would happen at 0%.

Other occasions were a little baffling, however. After the birth of our son I stayed at the hospital until 5 a.m., before driving home and sleeping for an hour, and then being woken up by our five-year-old daughter. It is safe to say I felt quite tired at that point, and both elated and emotionally drained at the same time. I don't think I could have got up and gone for a run, but Whoop told me I was 96% recovered. Often I would wake up feeling pretty good and see a recovery score of 30%, which didn't stop me from running, but did sow a seed of doubt in my mind and make me question my ability to decide how I was feeling for myself.

In order to try to understand more about how HRV works, I spoke to Dr Marco Altini, an Italian data scientist, author of over 50 publications on technology, health and performance, who has developed his own app to measure HRV. The simplest way of thinking about HRV, he says, is as 'a proxy for stress'. It is possible to measure stress at a hormonal level, but not in a reliable or practical way. Monitoring the autonomic nervous system is much easier and this is what HRV attempts to capture – variations in heart rhythms in response to stress.

The problem with the way in which wearable technologies represent this is that they don't know the context in which the reading has been made – there is no way, obviously, for the app to know that you just witnessed something hugely significant like the birth of your son, but nor does it have other vital information. 'The interpretation is extremely simplistic,' Marco says of the HRV reading: 'It's higher, so it's better.' A high HRV score will trigger the app to tell you, 'Hey it's high, so go out and kill it,' as Marco puts it. But in reality, this same reading could be a result of your nervous system being especially active due to extreme fatigue. What this means is that your HRV could be high when you're extremely tired, in which case the app is programmed to give you precisely the wrong advice.

Whilst HRV can be measured relatively accurately through sensors on the wrist, especially when you're asleep, Marco is keen to emphasise that the data on sleep stages should be viewed as estimates. 'The accuracy is something like 60% for distinguishing between sleep stages,' he says. 'It's not far off random numbers.' What happens then is that most devices combine these estimates with the HRV data, which ends up 'hiding the relevant information,' Marco explains.

He describes a scenario where someone starts training a little more and sleeping a little less. 'It could be that their physiology is actually great, because they've responded well and sleeping a bit less is not a problem for their body,' he says. 'But instead you have this algorithm that thinks these things should be negative for you and that's quite confusing.' I ask if he thinks that companies are deliberately trying to simplify the messages they send people. 'Of course, and that makes sense, we want everything to be simple,' he says. 'The problem, though, is that it is just inaccurate, so if people are a bit more serious about performance it becomes even less useful.'

What we end up with, then, is devices that are designed to satisfy our desire for simplicity and for being told what to do. I wonder what the overall effect of this is and what kind of training it pushes us towards. 'If you followed the advice these things give as to when to push hard in training and when to ease off,' I ask, 'do you think that would push everyone towards a kind of average?' Marco takes a few seconds to think about it and then says, 'I don't think so necessarily, but it would just be random training.'

It strikes me from talking to Kieran, for whom a large part of his motivation for running came from an interest in technological developments, that our relationship with these things has changed drastically in quite a short space of time.

When the first GPS devices came out they were chunky, triangular things that you had to strap to your bicep, and, as Kieran puts it, 'most people in the running community thought you were crazy' if you wore them. Now we have come full circle and running without a GPS watch is so unusual people refer to it as 'naked running'.

The no-nonsense approach to training which characterised the Gateshead Harriers in the 1980s – which I had mythologised as a teenager growing up in Durham – continues to have a pull for me. I wonder what that generation of runners would make of GPS watches, wearable technology and glucose monitoring, so I call Charlie Spedding. Luckily for me, Charlie lives a couple of streets away and I bump into him fairly regularly when he's out walking his dog, but I'm probably one of the few people who know that he's Britain's last Olympic medallist in the marathon.

We meet in the cash-only Colpitts pub and I sweat by the fire after a sprint to the ATM. Charlie's is a calm presence and he speaks thoughtfully, pausing frequently to ensure he's speaking with precision. I expect him to be quite dismissive of the introduction of so much new technology – after all, he ran his best marathon time of 2.08.33 many years before the GPS watch and the introduction of super shoes, and two years before I was born, in 1985. That time still leaves him seventh in the all-time British rankings, behind athletes including Mo Farah and Steve Jones (who also ran his best time in 1985). With the exception of Jones the others all wore the carbon fibre-plated shoes that have revolutionised road running, and three of the times are from 2024.

I show him the Whoop app and explain how Supersapiens works, but we start our discussion with the more ubiquitous

Garmin watches and heart rate monitors. 'Would you have used them if they were available when you were running?' I ask.

'I think so, yes,' Charlie says, drumming his fingers on the table. 'In certain circumstances and for certain training sessions. I'd stopped competing when they were introduced, but I think they would have been useful for what are now called threshold runs. That terminology didn't exist when I was running, but I started doing that kind of run on feel later in my career and I think using heart rate for those runs would have been beneficial.'

'So how did you judge the pace of those runs when you were competing?' I ask.

'It's a pace that's just pulled back from running as hard as you can,' he says. 'So if you could use a heart rate monitor on that specific run to avoid going too hard I could see that being useful.'

I am curious about this, because so much of what I've heard about Gateshead Harriers was about the importance of the group environment for helping people to improve. I ask about what those harder runs were like when he did them.

'It was in the late seventies that I first started going through to Gateshead every Tuesday night to run with a big group,' he says. 'We'd do a 10-mile run at a decent pace and often there would be three or four longer efforts thrown in at agreed points along the route. They were probably about a mile and they would have been well under five-minute-mile pace. Definitely. How fast I don't know, but they were pretty hard.' I'd heard about these runs from my own coach Max. The Tuesday night training run was so well-known it was even televised at one point in the early eighties, and I'd often wished I could time-travel back there and run in that group as a teenager.

'So they were tough, tough sessions,' Charlie goes on, 'but they were made easier by having six, seven, sometimes eight guys who could all handle it running together. It was much easier than trying to do it by yourself. There was certainly an element of camaraderie there. I saw people like John Caine and Brendan Foster going off to the Commonwealth Games or the European Championships and stuff. I realised I was able to do these training runs with them and that raised my expectations. I've always thought that. If you wanted to be any good within the running club you had to be an international at that point. That was the kind of atmosphere we had.'

I am curious about this, because it seems to me that using heart rate monitors to dictate the pace of these group runs would render them impossible – after all, you can only run according to one person's heart rate. I've experienced this in the past running with people who train according to their heart rate. You'll be running along nicely and be tempted to push the pace a little up a bit of an incline, and then they'll turn to you and say something like, 'We'd better back off a bit. My heart rate is going to go over 160.' The flow of the run is interrupted, but so is the sense that it is a common and equal endeavour. If the Gateshead group had all run according to their own pre-determined heart rate zones, they'd have been spread out and lost the very group advantage the run was intended to cultivate.

'You'd have to do those specific heart rate-based runs on your own then?' I ask Charlie. 'Yes, I suppose you would,' he says. This, it seems to me, is part of the issue with a data-driven approach to thinking about endurance and our capabilities as athletes – it has the effect of making everything about the individual, and the more importance we place on our own data and understanding our bodies on a granular level, the more likely we are to look inwards rather than outwards towards others.

So Charlie might have used a heart rate monitor for one specific kind of run. He would have used a Garmin occasionally, but been careful to avoid wearing one all the time. 'I'd probably want to use them so I knew exactly how far a training route was, but then I'd want to just run that route feeling what pace I was going,' he says. He credits regular 20-mile runs with a group – often starting at Brendan Foster's house – which he started doing when he was in his early twenties, with giving him the endurance to later run so well at the marathon. I ask about the pace these runs were done at. 'It wasn't slow, but no-one was pushing it or racing it. They were all good runners, though, so it was a decent pace.'

'And did you have a way of knowing what pace you were going in terms of minutes per mile at that point?'

'Yes,' he says, emphatically. 'Feel.' He goes on, 'I think it's dangerous to get too dependent on a GPS watch. There's nothing wrong with using them sometimes, but one of the most important things as a distance runner is being able to just gauge your pace based on what it feels like. That was one of my real strengths as a runner and I could do it on the track as well. I could always hit a 400m rep to within one second based on feeling the pace.'

This seems like a very clear example of a situation where technology actually does precisely the opposite of giving us more insight into our bodies and a deeper understanding of ourselves. Rather, through relying on a watch and rejecting the cultivation of a 'feel' for pace, we are blunting our ability to know intuitively how we are feeling.

'Being a good competitor,' Charlie says, 'is about being able to make the right decision under pressure, when you're under physical pressure, because you're very close to the edge, and you're under the mental pressure of am I going to beat this guy or am I not? Am I going to win or am I not?' His eyes light up when he talks about these kinds of competitive battles.

'I think being able to make the right decision when you think: "This guy's going really hard, should I go with him or do I let him go?" Or: "We're both really tired, should I go past him to put the pressure on him to hope he breaks? All those things that are a bit of a risk and you've got to make a decision and you're under pressure doing it, technology doesn't help you with that. That comes from within and I think if you're constantly relying on technology you're not thinking like that.'

I tell him that the way he talks about using GPS watches is strikingly similar to the way the Ethiopian runners I know used them when they first arrived in the country. They often actively rejected using them for runs in the forest which were seen as being more rejuvenating or even creative.

'Exactly,' Charlie says. 'Some of those runs should be exactly that. I used to *love* running. Obviously not every time when you're training hard, because sometimes you're tired and you've just got home from work and you've got to go out in horizontal sleet in winter or whatever, but sometimes – often – I just *loved* it. And if I felt like I was measuring it precisely it wouldn't be the same thing. It was a joy, not something to think, "Oh, I could have done that faster."'

What devices like Whoop and the Oura ring claim to be particularly good at is helping people to monitor their background levels of fatigue and make decisions about how hard to train and when, so I'm keen to understand how Charlie used to judge that.

How did he know when to back off a bit and when he was too tired to train effectively?

'Well, I'll tell you one story,' he says. 'I was living in Durham and still racing on the track and the nearest synthetic track was Gateshead – there wasn't one at Chester-le-Street or Durham at the time. I had a specific session to do and I was doing it on my own, because there was no-one doing that particular kind of training at the time, so I drove through to Gateshead Stadium. I did a two-mile loop to warm up, went on to the track and changed into my spikes. I did a couple of laps of striding the straights and jogging the bends and I went up to the starting line and I thought' – and here he holds up his hands in a gesture of submission – 'I can't do this. I just can't do it.'

He shakes his head at the memory. 'That was quite rare for me,' he goes on. 'So I thought, I'll do another couple of laps of striding and jogging, and so I did that and again I thought I just can't do it. So I changed my shoes and put my tracksuit back on and I drove home. I thought, "I'm just too tired. I don't feel capable of doing the session." So apart from the couple of miles warm-up and the strides I had the afternoon off. I went back to the track the next day, did the session I was supposed to do and did it really well. It was just a feeling. It just took a little bit more rest.'

It could be that had Charlie had access to wearable technology like Whoop or Garmin the outcome would have been the same – he'd have woken up to see an unusually low HRV score, or a rock-bottom 'readiness' score on his Garmin, and have decided to push the session back a day. In fact, he'd probably have pushed a lot of track sessions back a day had he had access to this kind of data. But for him, the ability to make the decision for himself was extremely important.

'I've thought back to that quite often and felt quite pleased with myself, because I bailed out. Because normally you would say you shouldn't do that, you know, you're tired, get on with it. There were loads of times I'd come home from work and have to go out and run 10 miles and really not feel like it, but you go and once you've run a mile or two you're fine and you do it. But a track session, you've got to do it right or close to right, so I've always been pleased that I listened to my body. So that's just one very clear example, but listening to my body was something that I would do and I would skip a training run I was supposed to do if I was *really* too tired.'

'So it's about knowing the difference between tired and too tired?' I ask.

'Knowing the difference, yeah.' Charlie nods.

'But on a day-to-day basis you're aware of being really quite tired all the time?' I ask.

'Yeah, well you are,' he replies. 'When you're training hard you're tired all the time, and the occasions when I was doing the highest mileage I ever did, I just felt like I was running all the time. Even though the two runs you're doing in the day when you're doing your biggest spell of mileage are just a couple of miles longer each, which doesn't seem like much, when you've done a couple of weeks of it you start to think, "I'm out running *again.*" And you accept that and you accept being tired, but there's a line where you think, "No, what I need more is a rest." And I don't want a watch making that decision for me. Absolutely not.'

In Charlie's view, taking control of these kinds of decisions yourself is an important part of becoming an accomplished endurance athlete. You have to be able to feel where the edge is in particular training sessions, to have a sense of pace from the catch of your breath and the weight of your legs, and you have to be able to be attentive to the background fatigue that is the constant companion of any athlete. It is tempting to draw a straight line from that skipped training session in Gateshead to the decisions Charlie made in the glare and tumult of the LA Olympic marathon, firstly, to push the pace with a 4.49 21st mile in order to whittle down the group and, secondly, *not* to try to go with Carlos Lopes when he made his decisive move, a decision which could easily have seen him fall by the wayside along with the favourites, Rob de Castella and Toshihiko Seko.

Given the ubiquity of wearable technology and the advertising that surrounds it, it might come as a surprise that one of the minority of runners who wasn't wearing a GPS watch at the 2023 London Marathon also managed to run faster than Charlie did 38 years previously. Emile Cairess ran 26 seconds faster than Charlie and he did so wearing a Casio watch he borrowed from his girlfriend. In an interview with *Runner's World* he talks about the importance of being able to judge the pace of an 'easy' or 'steady' run on the basis of feeling alone: 'I have my routes and I know how far they are, so I do know my pace in the end, but while I'm running I've not really got any idea of the pace. I think it's good for you mentally to be a bit disengaged sometimes, rather than feeling stressed about things that don't need to be stressed about.'

It seems to me that one of the main benefits of running should be an escape from stress and an opportunity to 'disengage,' as Emile puts it. If we get too caught up in the minutiae of training paces, heart rate zones and other metrics, we're just replacing one set of stressors with another.

How these devices affect specific competitive encounters is perhaps even more interesting in professional cycling, where there are more metrics allowing people to calculate performance and riders spend much of their time staring at a computer that tells them their power output in real time. I decide to talk to Tao Geoghegan Hart about this, because I am curious about what happens when a rider has the kind of breakthrough performance he had in the 2020 Giro d'Italia, where he won the general classification or overall race, having not even started it as Ineos Grenadiers' team leader.

When we speak, Tao is sitting on the grass in glorious sunshine outside a rehab centre in Holland, where he is recovering from crashing out of the 2023 Giro. His face is framed by his knees as he squints down at the phone as I ask him about his first stage victory, which came at the ski-station finish at the top of Piancavallo following a 14km climb. 'We'd raced for about probably five and a half, five hours before the bottom of it,' he says, 'and we'd had a big day the day before, running for over 200km or so and finishing in the mountains. I remember a point where I saw some stuff on the screen and I was conscious of how high it had been for such a long time, and I kind of decided to tune out of it, because I think I knew I was feeling really good. And in some moments, you just have to trust your intuition and your feeling.'

The trouble with looking too closely at the numbers in that moment, he says, is that he 'would have expected the feeling of fatigue and exertion to come just from how high the power was,' which would have undermined his effort. It is usually the case that you fixate more on the numbers when it gets particularly hard, he says, which gives you a 'perception that the whole thing is harder than it is.' Often, once you get a chance to see the average output later, it is much lower than you thought.

'There will be moments in your career when you produce far more than you ever, ever thought was possible. It's a very interesting balance of using knowledge as power in terms of knowing what you can physically do, and then being able to surpass that because you know you're in peak condition,' he says. At some point on the Piancavallo, then, he decided he had to resist the temptation to look at the screen and just race. The time to really use the data to his advantage was on the following rest day, when the team were able to look closely at the numbers and see that the level on that 30-minute climb was as high as any rider on the team had ever reached.

'Those numbers don't lie,' he goes on, 'and it's good to see that confirmation of how high your level is, that you're not only at your best ever, but you know, the kind of limit of what has been done.' In this case, it was confirmation of what Tao already knew – that he tends to get better the longer and harder something gets – but it helped him to believe in himself as an athlete. In this case, then, the data can be tremendously empowering, allowing him to quickly recalibrate his expectations for the race.

As a professional, he is obviously very receptive to anything that might be beneficial to his career, and he uses lactate testing and Supersapiens glucose monitoring at particular points in the season. But he also thinks it's important to focus on the data that you can have most confidence in, so most days he only uses heart rate and power (his professional kit is more accurate than most mass market versions of the same devices, and measuring wattage is particularly reliable). 'It's so easy now to get pulled down a hundred different paths,' he says, 'and actually you see a lot of people lose focus on the bigger picture from being consumed by all of that.' Focusing on certain metrics that you know are going to be of benefit is the key, he says. 'I don't think there are many people in the world for whom having more and more numbers and datasets dictating how they live their lives is going to be beneficial.'

Our conversation turns to the less tangible influences on performance. There seems to be a lot going on in endurance sport – to do with motivation, emotional states, relationships to others – that can't be captured and quantified in this way. 'Anything that isn't quantifiable gets removed from the picture, because you don't want that disrupting your data set,' Tao says. 'But our emotions and our experiences as humans – we aren't robots – actually determine far more of our performance than anything else.'

He talks about the importance of the competitive encounter for bringing the kind of jumps in performance he made at the Giro. 'The dual purpose of that is you're not only competing with each other, but you're collaborating to raise the level,' he points out. 'To bring that level up the energy kind of comes from the other riders as well.' Surpassing the performances of your predecessors isn't just about the introduction of new technology, then, but about building the belief that new limits can be reached.

One consequence of the increased availability of data – especially power data – is that riders are bridging the gap between the junior and senior ranks much more quickly, in a case that Tao refers to as 'accelerated development'. In some ways this is reminiscent of the shift I observed in Ethiopia. Whereas previously athletes would have started out on the track, before gradually moving up in distance and running their first marathon in their late twenties or early thirties, now talented distance runners often go straight to the marathon at 18, a move which allows them to make money more quickly, but often accelerates and then curtails their careers due to injury or illness.

Tao suspects that something similar could happen in cycling. Whilst the traditional pathway in cycling would be you work for others, learn and slowly improve, and peak in your mid to late twenties, now you see riders making the jump out of the junior categories and into longer and more intense races far earlier. Whether this will have the same effect of shortening careers is unclear at this stage, but there are other things at stake, too. As Tao puts it, there's also the risk of 'not living as a young person and enjoying those key years in your own personal development.'

Keen to understand all of this better, I arrange a chat with Natasha Dow Schull, a fellow anthropologist who has been working on self-tracking and wearable technologies for the last few years. Her first book, *Addiction by Design*, examined the lure of slot machines in American casinos, looking at everything from the design of the carpets (no right-angles so people don't need to engage the decision-making part of their brains and question their decision to gamble, too) to the machines themselves, as well as those who are addicted to them. She is now applying the same meticulous approach to studying self-tracking, speaking to the designers of wearables and those who code the apps that keep so many of us enthralled, as well as a range of people who track their behaviour, from the casual Apple Watch wearer to the people designing their own technology.

When we finally arrange a time that works for me in Durham and her in New York, she speaks quickly, in long and intricate sentences, and I'm glad I'm recording the conversation. It is important to look at self-tracking from a variety of perspectives, because, as she puts it, 'there is a tendency [in academia] to represent all of this stuff as data capitalism or surveillance capitalism', in other words, just a way for big companies to make money by knowing about and watching you. 'I call it "plug and play" where you just take something like self-tracking and you just plug it into surveillance capitalism and just run it and there's a readymade interpretation.'

Approaching wearable technology as an anthropologist means going beyond these interpretations, which rely on the idea that we are unwittingly providing data about ourselves to corporations for profit or giving in completely to nefarious algorithms. It is important to take seriously the meaning that people are able to make through these technologies and the positive experiences many people have with them, whilst also being aware of some of the potential consequences of becoming overly reliant on them.

Sociologist Chris Till has written about the idea of 'exercise as labour', so when we wear a smartwatch or use a run or ride tracking app on our phone we are turning something that should be one of our few moments of freedom – potentially a time to unplug, to get away from it all and just *be* – into a form of literal work that generates revenue for companies like Garmin, and Strava, the most popular platform to upload GPS and other running and cycling data to. He points to a *Financial Times* study from 2014 which showed that the 20 most popular health and fitness apps were selling personal data to around 70 different companies.

I think privacy is a serious issue and it's one that until recently hasn't been taken particularly seriously by companies like Strava (only since 2021 have the start and end points of runs been hidden by default), but in hundreds of conversations with undergraduate students on my anthropology of sport course I have met very few people who are concerned by this. In fact, most admit to not being particularly curious about where the data generated from their activities ends up. Natasha has experienced the same with her students in New York and for the most part they are extremely relaxed about routine digital surveillance. 'They'll be like, "I guess I want Netflix to know my taste because then they direct me to the movies I like,"' she says.

Critical takes like those of Till tend, then, to play down the importance of the subjective experience of going for a run or a ride. For him, any run that produces data for someone else becomes labour, but what if not everyone feels like they are working? If the watch on your wrist buzzing every kilometre adds to the experience of being out – there is, after all, a rewarding feeling of control in knowing you're going the 'right' pace – then that's great. There is a huge range of ways of relating to data, from feeling like you are becoming a 'slave to the watch' to finding the constant feedback useful and developing a kind of citizen-scientist approach to training.

One of the things I am most keen to ask Natasha about is anxiety. In one of her articles she notes that the wearables industry targets customers who are 'unsure whether to trust their own senses, desires and intuitions as they make choices – when and what to eat and drink, when and how much to eat or rest.' These are concerns that are amplified for people who like to spend their time moving long distances, because getting these things wrong in an ultra-marathon, for example, can lead to disaster. But whilst we have access to more and more data, this might actually increase our anxiety, rather than lessening it. As UCLA professor Safiya Noble, who has written extensively on the power of algorithms, has put it, 'More data is not better analysis' and if we're not careful we can feel overwhelmed with too much information in sports that have the potential to be extremely simple.

When I spent 15 months living and training in Ethiopia alongside some of the best long-distance runners in the world, I was struck by their selective use of wearable technologies. Theirs was a running expertise built intuitively and passed on primarily body to body, without the constant barrage of information new runners are subjected to on platforms like X or Instagram. A GPS watch was useful for measuring particular sessions where it was important to have precise information, but other kinds of running were seen as requiring a different kind of measurement of intensity.

Wearable devices, as well as apps like Strava, are actively designed to work against this kind of use, however. Just as we are increasingly expected to be always on – constantly connected to work, never quite switching off – we are sold the idea that our data is useless if it is incomplete, that we need to be plugged in at all times. As Natasha puts it, 'The mantra of any kind of consumer-digital interactive consumer experience is to remove friction.' Remember the casino carpets, carefully designed so you don't stop to second-guess the decision you've made to mindlessly pull a lever in a darkened room? In much the same way, many devices are moving away from just providing information to directing your behaviour. The personalised nutrition programme Zoe, for instance, not only provides blood glucose testing, but also specific meal plans.

Natasha studies a wide range of technologies, from wearables like the Oura ring to headsets and 'posture regulators' like Spire, which use 'haptics' – a buzz, for example – to tell you to modify your posture. She has traced a broad shift in thinking about these things from what she calls a 'compass logic' to a 'sentinel logic'. In the early days, she says, 'You'd see somebody in a parking lot or in a mall or somewhere holding their Fitbit or their device and looking at it, thinking, "Let me digest this information with my eyes in the mode of a compass and then make a decision myself about where to go or what to eat or do next."' She argues that many companies are now steering us away from this engaged approach to our data in favour of getting us to blindly follow 'nudges'. What she calls 'sentinel logic' often works through haptics rather than visual informatics. For instance, she says, 'You're typing at your office and maybe you're wearing a Spire posture regulator, and it'll buzz and you'll straighten your back, but you *will not stop typing.*' In this understanding, devices stand watch for our distracted and overwhelmed selves, offering nudges that keep us on track and – crucially – keep us working without reflecting on what we are doing.

Clearly many runners and cyclists have a far more active relationship with the data related to their sport than this – we tend to use devices in the 'compass' mode – but it is still possible to see a shift towards a more prescriptive approach from companies like Whoop and Supersapiens. When I get a notification from Whoop at 8 p.m. telling me I should 'get ready for bed in order to maximise my sleep performance' for instance, or an e-mail on New Year's Eve entitled 'How long does alcohol stay in your system' I can't avoid the feeling that I'm somehow being reprimanded. In a recent survey I was sent by Supersapiens, one of the questions was about whether as a customer I would be interested in 'specific meal plans and personalised content', which other companies like Zoe are already providing. Clearly, Supersapiens was looking to retain and ultimately expand its market share, but again I couldn't quite shake the sense that it was potentially being somewhat controlling.

For Natasha, the endurance community (people actively engaged in running, cycling and triathlon) are still in what she calls the 'meaningful insight' stage of our relationship with data. From what she sees in her research, we're engaged and able to reflect on things like HRV scores and GPS information critically, which is just as well given the inaccuracies I've described. However, she emphasises that there is 'a dominant desire on the part of the general public to say, "Just track it for me."' It's also a 'dominant desire' for those designing these products, I'd have thought, for whom the important thing is that you feel like you need to keep using them all the time (Whoop even has a detachable charger so the strap itself never has to leave your wrist).

So is this the future we want – Zoe telling us exactly what to eat and when, Whoop telling us when to go to bed, and Strava telling us the optimum training run for a particular day? Because from my perspective there is something to be said for working these things out for yourself, or at least being able to seriously deliberate on the basis of what you are told and what you feel. For Natasha, it is important that we continue to interrogate the data produced by these devices, rather than blindly following it, and there are still plenty of ways to do this effectively – a return to an old-fashioned training diary, for example, or conversations with a coach or other runners.

In fact, I also want to consider how our reliance on data impacts our relationships with others. In posts about the benefits of remote coaching, we now see arguments in favour of using large amounts of data from wearables in order to remove the need for a coach to be present at a training session. Indeed, for some proponents of this approach, the coach being there and interacting with the athlete introduces too much 'subjectivity' to the decision-making process. One online coach writes, 'I can tell athletes that in their speed sessions as they fatigued their stride length shortened.' According to this particular coach, this kind of insight can be more 'effective' than actually seeing a coach at the track, because by not being there they can be more objective in their use of data.

What might the future hold if this trend towards datafication continues? We might imagine AI running coaches supplanting the online coach above (who would, in turn, become too subjective). These would be fed various forms of data, from GPS tracking to glucose levels and the amount of lactic acid in the blood. They might tell you the optimum time to go to bed and exactly how long to sleep for, and tailor an individualised training programme to your precise needs. Perhaps they will tell you which heart rate zone you should be in for each training run you do, and administer a brief electric shock whenever you err from it.

All of this might, in one sense, optimise performance. But it's easy to imagine how such highly individualised solutions would have consequences for our social lives and relationships. Reading these kinds of posts about remote coaching makes me think about a time when I suggested to my own coach in the middle of marathon training that I do sessions on my own to make it easier to fit them into a busy day. His response was unequivocal. 'No. I need to be able to see the whites of your eyes,' was how he put it. By this he meant he had to be able to closely monitor how hard I was working, but he also meant more than that. You need to be able to have the peripheral conversations about the difficult boss, upcoming house move or whatever is on your mind at the time. In short, you need a relationship that goes beyond the sport, so that you know when and how to tell someone to take a day off or skip the last rep.

By making everything about extremely specific metrics – be that heart rate zone at the moment or lactic threshold when mobile testing becomes more efficient – we also run the risk of individualising training to the extent it actually becomes very difficult to run with others, especially if they also have a remote coach who dictates each run in very specific terms. All of this is strikingly different to the way the Ethiopian runners I knew trained, none of whom were interested in heart rate zones or knew what their lactic threshold was. For them, 'measuring' themselves was a social activity that involved seeing how they were doing in relation to their teammates.

In a sense this is because they were all aiming to get to roughly the same level – they needed to be able to run a marathon in around two hours and six minutes if they wanted to be able to 'change their lives' through the sport. So they had to train at paces that would get them to that (extremely high) level, even if it meant sometimes having to jump on the bus halfway through sessions or spend months barely hanging on in every run. This is a wildly different approach that clearly comes down to the value placed on the group environment over individual specialisation.

This would seem to be the case in Kenya as well. Reflecting on the difference between coaching Kenyan athletes and the many foreign runners who go to train at altitude in Iten, the famous base for Kenyan runners, the Italian coach Renato Canova talks about the different approaches taken to modifying training sessions that are too hard. He gives the example of telling runners to do an hour of hard running at a pace of just over three minutes per kilometre. The Kenyan athletes he coaches would run together at the pace he told them to run and either survive it or stop after 40 minutes or so when they started to let the pace slip. But if the European athletes didn't think they could run the pace, they would calculate what pace they thought they *could* hold for an hour and do that on their own. One of these approaches may well be better in terms of the physiological effects of the training session, but perhaps there are other things that are worth thinking about, too.

4

TO THE SUN

It is the evening of 25 June, we are somewhere just north of Ecclefechan in the Scottish borders, and for the first time in 25 miles it is just Ben and I, rolling hills and the dramatically fading light. The official time from dusk until dawn is only four hours and 39 minutes tonight, and we will be spending that time riding to the sea at Cramond on the outskirts of Edinburgh. We have just come through a brief shower and now bulbous grey clouds loom above us, whilst the horizon is streaked with rays of sunlight. Soon, the sky to our right turns a deep blue-grey, which contrasts sharply with the vivid green of the fields. 'Well, this is quite nice,' Ben points out – and it is.

I like that we are riding north for the solstice, spending the night on our bikes in order to see the sun rise a few minutes earlier than it would have done where we started. I am intrigued to see how dark it will get, and keen to pay attention to the night as it falls and the morning as it breaks. As an anthropologist I am perhaps primed to look for elements of the ritualistic, but this does seem to have more of the ritual to it than more conventional endurance events. It feels important that we are doing this on the solstice, enacting a kind of moving vigil on the shortest night. It seems significant to mark the changing seasons with something challenging that brings together a bunch of people who wouldn't otherwise know each other.

For a ride that is only 'organised' in a loose sense, without sign-up fees or race numbers, I am surprised to find that almost a thousand people are riding tonight. Various groups of riders have formed and disbanded organically over the last couple of hours, and we've been riding with 10 to 20 people most of the way so far. We ride for a while with two guys who used to do 24-hour endurance rides when they were in high school, for whom this was presumably a comparatively short ride. 'What made you want to ride for 24 hours?' I ask one of them. 'I have no idea,' comes the response. 'We were just ballsy teenagers.' They head off up the road and we are joined by an older guy in Royal Marines Lycra. 'I've been retired a long time,' he says, 'so I like to do this sort of thing every now and then just to keep myself on my toes.'

The 25-mile mark for me, however, is already unknown territory on a bike. After my time in the Sierra Rarámuri I was intrigued by the concept of taking part in endurance events without training for them in any specific way. If a large part of participating in these kinds of experiences is about venturing into the unknown and putting yourself in a situation where you are not completely sure how your body and mind will react, then heading to the start line almost completely untrained surely adds to the intrigue. Whilst I have been doing quite a lot of running, the extent of my cycling for the last year has been one 90-minute gravel ride and the daily mile and a half to school with my daughter.

When I expressed my concerns about this to Ben he was dismissive. 'You'll be fine,' he said. 'You just need to eat a lot and keep pedalling.' My main worry for the first hour or so had therefore been keeping down the enormous burger I'd eaten in Carlisle, having taken advantage of the new phenomenon of calories on menus to order by quantity rather than quality. I'm also conscious of remaining as attentive as possible to the riders around me. It feels brilliant to be moving together in such a big group, but it's not something I'm used to on the bike and I'm keen to avoid causing an accident.

There is no start time for the Ride to the Sun, so participants are free to work out for themselves roughly when they should start in order to reach Cramond by dawn. This means that we periodically pass riders who have set out earlier and other groups come past us moving a bit more quickly. There is no sense of competitiveness at all, but the years I've spent approaching endurance sport as racing mean it is hard to shake off thoughts like, 'Maybe I could just hang on to this guy for a bit as he goes past' or 'We need to break up this group a bit soon.' No, I have to remind myself: we need to enjoy being here and the more company we have the easier 100 miles will be.

In his historical account of 'keeping together in time', the American historian William H McNeil writes about the importance moving together has had for creating social bonds. His focus is mainly on dancing and military drill – synchronised marching on parade grounds and during war – but he argues that 'moving our muscles rhythmically [...] consolidates human solidarity by altering human feelings.' Most people know this intuitively from experience, he writes, and yet it is 'little discussed by any learned discipline.' Recalling 'strutting around' for hours as part of military drill, he writes:

Words are inadequate to describe the emotion aroused by the prolonged movement in unison that drilling involved. A sense of pervasive well-being is what I recall; more specifically, a strange sense of personal enlargement; a sort of swelling out, becoming bigger than life, thanks to participation in collective ritual.

There is something visceral and timeless about this sense of togetherness that movement creates, something 'far older than language', and McNeil speculates that it is difficult to articulate because we respond to rhythmic movement primarily through the sympathetic and para-sympathetic nervous systems, which are responsible for the subconsciously maintained rhythms of our hearts, digestive systems and breathing. 'The initial seat of excitement,' as he puts it, 'is far removed from our verbal capacities.' Much of McNeil's book is concerned with dance and he notes that communal dancing across many societies is associated with experiences of 'boundary loss' where individuals feel at one with each other, and a heightened sense of fellow-feeling. If you've ever been to a ceilidh you might have had a taste of this.

Anthropologists have a range of terms for exploring the powerful effects of this kind of communal feeling. Writing about the Andaman Islands in the early 20th century, AR Radcliffe-Brown wrote that, 'As the dancer loses himself in the dance, as he becomes absorbed in the unified community, he reaches a state of elation in which he feels himself filled with energy or force immediately beyond his ordinary state, and so finds himself able to perform prodigies of exertion.' I'm not convinced, trundling along at the back of our group of 20 or so riders, that I'm about to perform any 'prodigies of exertion', but I do know that this feels a lot easier in the group, and that there is already a powerful and immediate sense of fellow-feeling amongst a collection of riders who have never met each other in their lives.

The statement would also resonate with the Ethiopian runners I trained with, though – and they certainly *were* capable of prodigious displays of endurance. Running in a group was very much seen as a way of collectively producing performances that could not be achieved alone. It is an example of what the French sociologist Emile Durkheim called 'collective effervescence' in his work on religion at the beginning of the 20th century: an intensification of shared experience and emotional energy that is reinforced by rhythmic bodily movement. The notion of collective energy has often been disparaged as imprecise or 'mystical' language, because it is often so intangible. To the runners I knew, though, the effects of collective effervescence were clear and visible to all, and objectively measurable in the times they were able to run.

This kind of collective running was not necessarily considered to come easily to people in Ethiopia, though, and I am keen not to rehearse a tired contrast between the individualistic 'West' and more co-operative elsewhere. Anthropological work on the Amhara, the ethnic group the vast majority of runners I knew belonged to, has in fact revealed a strong tendency to characterise people as selfish and individualistic, often requiring legal and religious constraints in order to work together. In a way this awareness, combined with the hyper-competitive environment of Ethiopian running, actually brings people together. Runners know that they need each other in order to improve and they also know that working together requires constant effort.

When I ran in Ethiopia the power of collective running was recognised and respected, and people orchestrated these moments carefully, making sure that pace-making responsibilities were evenly divided amongst the runners. There was a clear sense that a runner could only realise their ambitions by being part of a collective, which is also true of other religious and social celebrations of togetherness in Ethiopia. Yet entering into this kind of running was also understood to require a form of trust between runners that had to be worked on constantly, and these moments had to be prepared for specifically and meticulously.

I wasn't expecting to learn anything about running when I visited the Fendika Azmari Bet, a bar in Addis Ababa where singers play traditional string instruments, with my partner Roslyn. We were there to listen to music and drink *tej*, a sweet honey wine that is served in a transparent gourd that looks more like a piece of chemistry equipment than a glass. *Tej* gets you drunk from the feet up, as I discovered when we tried to leave after several hours and my legs seemed to have a mind of their own. The Azmari Bet offers a fascinating blend of folk songs and stand-up comedy, and we were the subject of quite a few Amharic jokes as we watched the dancers perform.

In spite of this distraction I was struck by the similarities between the traditional *eskesta* dancing and the warm-up routines which we used to follow before we started our training runs. Both involved rhythmic movement that emphasised bringing the feet down on to the ground in time, and even the synchronising of sharp inhalations and exhalations, which is an important feature of the dancing. Both started more slowly and built towards a crescendo as the energy of the group was harnessed and put to work. And both, crucially, were *fun* – the smiles that spread on the faces of the dancers mirrored those of the runners towards the end of a long warm-up routine of synchronised exercises, who found themselves now awake, alert and ready to run together.

The warm-up, then, seems to be as much about bringing people together as a social group and producing common feeling as it is about priming the muscular and nervous systems. It makes the training session itself into a particular kind of event, which we might characterise as a sort of ritual, and this was also how I was tempted to think about our overnight ride to Cramond. In Victor Turner's classic work on ritual, there is a 'liminal' period which temporarily transports people beyond their routine lives, to a 'moment in and out of time', where they are removed from their usual social status, and the usual hierarchies and distinctions that characterise their lives are broken down.

Turner explored the idea of a 'liminal period' primarily through studies of African rites of passage, particularly amongst the Ndembu people in Zimbabwe. Many Ndembu rituals involve role reversal, for instance where the crown-elect and other powerful figures are made to take on the role of commoners, and can be degraded and insulted in a way that they couldn't be in everyday life. 'What is interesting about liminal phenomena,' Turner writes, is 'the blend they offer of lowliness and sacredness, of homogeneity and comradeship.' Rites of passage of this kind, he goes on, reveal, 'however fleetingly' some recognition of a generalised social bond.

For Turner the 'liminal' period is the second of three ritual phases. The first is a separation from normal life and the last is a re-incorporation into everyday life accompanied by some shift in social norms or status. He has been criticised for over-emphasising the power of ritual to genuinely lead to new kinds of social status, but it seems to me there is some transformative potential in bringing people together in this way. Turner refers to the common feeling engendered by participating in these kinds of rituals together as 'communitas'. Furthermore, and perhaps most relevant to thinking about endurance events as rituals, he writes that rituals are characterised by the *acceptance of pain and suffering*.

As I ride along, musing happily about the power of ritual and moving together in a non-competitive way, I suddenly notice there has been a slight change in the group. We're not far from Moffat now and the couple in front of us have started muttering about the chip shop queue. There is light-hearted joking about this and then one of them takes off up the road. Ben grins, clearly keen for a bit of a race. I send him up the road and, like a faithful domestique, he heads off in pursuit to order two fish suppers.

When I arrive the queue for the chippy reaches halfway down the high street, but Ben is somehow already inside. There are so many bikes lining the high street that most people have opted to lean them precariously against each other. I find a wall to perch on and watch as more riders stream into town. For a more eccentric event there is still a lot of Lycra on display and some very expensive bikes, but there are also plenty of people riding commuter bikes and old racing bikes from the eighties. It is still light at about 9 p.m. and a girl who can't be older than 12 arrives with her dad, who rides in a checkered shirt, an unzipped high-vis vest flapping around him. Behind them a couple who must be in their seventies refill water bottles from a huge barrel.

By the time we leave Moffat to climb the wonderfully named Devil's Beef Tub it is dusk and I've just eaten my second huge meal in about three hours. We couldn't have arrived at the hill at a better time, though, because as we snake slowly up the slope we join a line of hundreds of riders, their lights shining under a blue-grey sky. Towards the top of the hill it looks like a chain of fairy lights are being slowly draped across the horizon. We ride steadily – after all, from the top there are still 50 miles to go – and I find an enjoyable rhythm, just keeping the pedals spinning without too much effort. Ben is a much better cyclist than me, but he's clearly content to ride up the hill side by side.

I can't remember all of what we talk about, but I'm conscious of feeling like we're having a better catch-up than we have in years, since we used to live together as students in Edinburgh. It's difficult, after all, to find the time for a drawn-out nine-hour chat under normal circumstances. Conversations whilst riding, running or walking are different, too. They are without the pressure of other kinds of interaction – side by side there is little eye contact and no requirement to respond immediately. This is especially true at certain paces. If you are riding up a hill, even at an easy cadence, there are natural pauses where you are breathing slightly too heavily to talk and a pause for thought is easily disguised as a pause for breath.

There are also long periods of silence, both of us quite happy to enjoy the fading light on the hillside and the easy rhythm of our uphill pedalling. Moving together like this provides a space for being-with, or being-alongside someone, where silence is completely acceptable. Writing about hill walking and the increasing difficulty of finding silence in nature, the great chronicler of life in the mountains Nan Shepherd considers the ideal walking companion to be someone who is comfortable with silence, who enhances rather than detracting from it.

For Shepherd, it was important to walk with people who enjoyed, as she did, merging their identities with the mountain itself. She liked to walk with people who understood that talk for the sake of it could ruin this experience. This might be why I often find myself having quite deep conversations during long runs and bike rides – small talk feels like a waste of breath and an insult to the silence. This ideal that she describes, of becoming part of the environment, also makes intuitive sense. It feels to me that this is amplified through exertion, that through working hard we are thinning the membrane between ourselves and the world, running or riding ourselves transparent.

We reach the top of the climb at 10.30 p.m. and there is still plenty of light in the surrounding hills, which fall away on both sides of the road in green pleats. A small crowd is gathered at the summit around a lone kilted piper, who plays rousing music to welcome the new arrivals. We linger awhile before starting our descent and as night falls it suddenly starts to absolutely hose it down with rain, turning the road slick and the air freezing. As it gets darker I realise that in the absence of any street lights my bike lights are extremely poor and clearly designed so that cars can see me, rather than so that I can see the road. I am therefore quite reliant on Ben with his better lighting and night vision to avoid ending up in the ditch.

The rain gets so hard at one point that my field of vision is reduced to a splattered and squinty pool of light, and I hunch over the handlebars and try to stay close to Ben on the long descent. It's amazing how quickly I go from feeling warm and elated to wondering how long my frozen fingers will be able to hold on to the handlebars. In spite of this I am still musing about endurance events and ritual. There is only so far that we can push a comparison between the decision of a random group of people to spend a night cycling to Scotland and the Ndembu rituals Victor Turner writes about, but it does occur to me that events like this can have a similar levelling effect.

I am in danger of losing all the feeling in my fingers until Ben lends me his spare gloves and later I hear about others who have been rescued by a loaned raincoat or a spare pair of waterproof trousers. At some level, for the brief period in which we are drenched to the bone and at slight risk of hypothermia, we are all suffering together. Writing in 1995, McNeil notes that bonding through exercise seems to have been an 'important cement for human communities in times past' and that our neglect of these ways of connecting with each other today represents a significant departure from the past. The need for community is especially acute in 'big anonymous cities' he adds, which is perhaps even more true today than it was 30 years ago.

It is funny that I've been thinking about McNeil's writing on dance as we ride, because when we finally arrive at the Tweed Inn in Tweedsmuir just before midnight we are greeted by a rain-soaked and quite surreal scene. Lycra clad and slightly dazed cyclists mill around beside endless crates of bananas and a DJ presides over a small outdoor dancefloor. Over the unmistakeable intro to Fatboy Slim's 'Right Here, Right Now' the climate campaigner Greta Thunberg's barely contained rage fills the carpark: 'The eyes of all future generations are upon you. We will not let you get away with this. Right here, right now is where we draw the line…'

The throbbing bass and righteous fury of Thunberg's voice sends a shiver down my spine that has little to do with the freezing rain. A lot of people are wearing cycling cleats, so the 'rhythmic movement' that unfolds can perhaps only loosely be described as dancing, but we nevertheless shuffle and bob to the music, trying, as much as anything else, to warm up after the long and soaking descent. Ben and I eat the flapjacks my partner and daughter baked for us and, once we're out of the wind, gradually start to feel less cold. We are over halfway now and the rest of the journey should be gently downhill.

Early in the ride I was very conscious of the distance and of my complete lack of cycling 'miles in the legs'. I was very mindful of keeping my legs as fresh as possible by spinning a very light gear and resisting any urge to ride more quickly, keep up with someone faster or try to catch up with someone ahead. In this first part of the ride I think a lot, making constant micro-decisions about effort and my positioning on the bike, and trying to evaluate exactly how I'm feeling relative to how far I still have to ride. I don't have any way of knowing how fast we are riding in kilometres an hour, but try to keep quite a keen sense of whether or not we are going at about the right pace – steady but easy to maintain.

At some time in the night, though, all this goes out of the window. Through a combination of the almost complete darkness, which makes it hard to judge how fast you are moving, and my basic exhaustion, I reach a place where my brain can only compute two things: staying upright and keeping going. This seems to happen at some stage in most of these endurance challenges. There comes a point of no return, a point at which you are either all in or you're sitting on the roadside.

From the many interviews I have done with people who take part in this kind of event it seems that achieving this state is a large part of their motivation. People speak of 'stripping things back' and the complete dropping away of extraneous concerns. This is also, I think, the truly 'liminal' aspect of these events, where we go somewhere else, into a new state of being, in order to return again, rejuvenated. There are moments when I'm in something of a trance and close to nodding off on the bike.

Luckily there are a few more surreal moments to keep me awake. We go through a small town just after 2 a.m., which must be when the local club kicks everyone out. Ben and I have just joined a big group of about 30 riders and as we whir past together, the inebriated and incredulous looks on people's faces – and some of the heckles – make the whole night worth it. A couple of hours later we navigate through the outskirts of Edinburgh using the tiny printout of instructions Ben has taped to his handlebars in lieu of any GPS technology, encountering more clubbers on their way home, who all seem to be wondering whether this many cyclists can really all have got up so early.

A little while after the ride I arrange a Zoom call with Fraser Maxwell and Gary Cameron, who founded and organise the Ride to the Sun, and both are keen to emphasise the event's organic evolution. 'The way it started was that Fraser was training to do an Ironman,' Gary begins. 'You know, your classic paid-for event, expensive, that kind of thing, and he was struggling to get in enough training to do it.' Fraser had young children at the time and he'd come up with a way of fitting in a big ride without being out all day – by being out all night instead. He says, 'I'd always fancied doing the Devil's Beef Tub climb and I needed a big ride in my legs and fancied a bit of an overnight adventure, so I asked a few people if they fancied it and everyone was like, "No that's a bit of a weird thing to do," but Gary being Gary was like, "Yeah, that sounds magic. I'll do that."' Gary is laughing.

It was only as they rode towards Moffat that they began to wonder whether it might work as a larger event. 'When we got to the chippy we said to the lady there, "We've got this crazy idea for a bike ride. Would you be up for staying open for it?" and straight away she was like, "Yeah, brilliant, that sounds great,"' Gary says. 'That was a bit of a catalyst – if someone who had no interest in cycling thought it could work then we should give it a try.' That first year one of their mates came out of their house in Cramond with a six-pack. The next year a few more people came along – 'That was the year of the wheelbarrow' – says Fraser. By year three they realised they were going to need a bigger supply of beers and they'd outgrown the wheelbarrow, and now Stewarts brewery drops off enough free beer for hundreds of riders. 'They've bought into the ethos as well,' as Fraser puts it.

Most of the time they don't use the word 'event' to describe Ride to the Sun – it is a 'happening' or, to borrow from one of their friends, a 'flash mob'. 'I love the idea that there are hundreds of folk down at Cramond at 5 a.m., but by 7 a.m. someone walking their dog would have no idea that anything happened.' They are both keen to emphasise the importance of keeping the ride non-competitive and of making it as inclusive as possible. People have ridden the 100-mile route on Bromptons and fat bikes, and in brogues and cords. The ethos of the event is in conscious opposition to something like Ironman, which ironically was what inspired Fraser to trial the route in the first place.

'That first ride was in some ways just a means to an end,' Fraser says. He was short of time and he needed the miles. 'In an Ironman you're focused on the clock and you're thinking constantly about performance, but on that overnight ride we had bats flying across the sky, you're seeing deer running out in front of your lights, you've got badgers running along the side of the road and I saw a barn owl at the top of the Devil's Beef Tub. For me it's the antithesis of any kind of competitive event.'

I'm curious about the significance of holding the ride on the solstice, but this turns out to have been coincidence as much as anything. 'It's funny how you kind of build the meaning in afterwards,' says Fraser. The logo for the ride is a Roman Centurian's helmet, because it occurred to them afterwards that both Carlisle and Cramond were garrison towns, and they refer to Sol Invictus, the god of the unconquered sun, but these levels of meaning have gradually been added and participants are free to make up their own.

I tell them that part of the attraction of the event for me is that Ride to the Sun attempts to retain a sense of adventure when many endurance events seem to be about sanitising the experience as much as possible. There are no route markings, for instance, and if something goes wrong you are mostly reliant on other participants to help you fix a puncture or hand you an emergency sausage roll. This seems to bring people together, though, in a way that would be less possible in a paid-for event. 'If you look at all the feedback we've had over the years, the most common word that crops up is probably camaraderie,' Fraser says. 'There's something about the randomness of conversations that you spark up when you're riding along with someone you don't know and I always love the finish of the ride with everyone on the seafront swapping stories.'

When Ben and I finally do get down to Cramond – a small island in the Firth of Forth – it's around 4 a.m. and we take a couple of cans of beer down to the sea wall and sit down, looking out over the glassy expanse of the sea towards the island. Next to us, a guy in a battered old cycling cap is rolling a cigarette from a small stash of tobacco and papers he has stored in an old puncture repair kit. 'I gave up smoking years ago,' he says as he licks the paper, 'but I allow myself to smoke a couple after a big ride.' It turns out he rode down from Edinburgh to Carlisle yesterday before turning round and riding back overnight. 'I think you deserve it,' I say.

The hardest bit of the ride turns out to be the bit I hadn't considered: the eight miles back to Ben's flat on the other side of Edinburgh. By the time we make our way back to our bikes we've been sitting on the cold sea wall for a couple of hours and had another few beers each. It is now fully light and we ride slowly along the coast, past morning runners and dog walkers. My legs have more or less completely seized up by now, and it seems to take forever to get back to Piershill and drag the bikes up three flights of stairs.

When I wake up, shortly before midday, I find that initially I haven't the faintest idea where I am. When I try to move it feels like I've been beaten up, my entire body aching from over-exerting my muscles to such a degree. I've only been asleep for three or four hours and it feels less like I've been asleep than I've been temporarily extinguished completely. I think of the way my friend Paul Burgum, who is completing his PhD in psychology at Durham, speaks about ultra-marathons as a way of performing a kind of factory reset, both mentally and physically. Paul has completed numerous multi-day ultra-marathons, as well as participating in expeditions in the Arctic, and writes about endurance and resilience.

In both his own experience and from the research he has conducted, it seems an important part of these kinds of challenges is the fresh perspective they give on the rest of life. He talks about 'scraping off the life pollution' over the course of an endurance challenge, where everything pales into insignificance except the desire to continue, and then of the feeling of calm that can last for weeks afterwards. By the time I get back to work on Monday morning I am tired, of course, but at the same time the weekend feels like it has been strung out, like I've put more distance than usual between this week and last. Which, in a sense, I suppose I have.

5

LAKES IN A DAY

Not for the first time in the course of writing this book I am driving to meet a man I have never met before in a car park. Andy Berry has had some year, setting the fastest known time for a Winter Tranter's Round, a circuit which takes in 18 Munros (Scottish mountains over 3000 feet), before breaking the Lake District 24-hour record by covering 78 peaks (and some 94 miles, with 40,000 feet of ascent) in just over 23 hours. For good measure, he has just won the Lakeland 100, only taking the lead for the first time in the race in the final mile. Perhaps the most impressive thing about all this is that Andy lives and works in Durham which, whilst hilly, is not exactly the perfect place to prepare for record-breaking exploits in the mountains.

It is the first time, to Andy's knowledge, that the Lake District 24-hour record has been held by someone who doesn't live in the mountains. I'm hoping, then, that I might get a few tips on how to train for Lakes in a Day, a race I've entered which is exactly what it sounds like: you run across the whole of the Lake District – 50 miles from top to bottom – in a day. When I pull into the Hamsterley Forest car park at 6.45 a.m. the only other vehicle is a van, with two collies racing around it. I assume, rightly, that this is Andy's. As we head on to the trails it is clear the dogs know where they're going. Occasionally they will turn around, heads cocked, for Andy to confirm that we're heading on to a particular patch of single track, but for the most part they are in the lead.

We've planned to run for about two hours, before Andy, who is a plumber, heads to work. I start the voice recorder on my phone and it quickly becomes apparent that we could talk all day, the conversation meandering with the paths and ebbing and flowing with the hills. After about an hour he asks me if I have any specific questions or if I just want to 'talk around things', which is a nice way of putting it. Often the most interesting conversations happen this way anyway. As Lindsey Freeman puts it, on long easy runs it is often the case that 'thoughts and ideas do not usually sharpen to a point, but rather spool out like a cassette tape gone rogue.' This is a beautiful way of describing it and asking too many direct questions would hamper the unspooling of ideas. I do tell him, though, that I'm interested in exploring why it is that people want to do things like spend 24 hours running round the mountains.

'I think we're bored,' he says emphatically. 'If you look at places where people still have to fight to survive, whether that's collecting water or fighting disease or whatever, you don't tend to see them out doing stupidly long runs in the mountains.' He goes on: 'We've got the same brains we had 500 years ago – evolution takes a long time – and certain sections of society need to have that sense of challenge. I feel most alive when I'm out racing. We weren't built to be shoved behind a desk for the majority of our lives. I don't see how that's helpful for the human condition. It's become all about the trappings of it all. People are encouraged to buy a bigger house and then you need the pay rise to pay for it. You get the pay rise so then you're encouraged to buy the bigger car…'

'I suppose running's a bit like that too, though,' I counter. 'You do a 5km and think, "Maybe I can do a 10km" and then you're encouraged to do a marathon.' He laughs. 'Yeah and then it's like, "Now I can do a 50-miler." Absolutely. A lot of people get lulled into that I guess.' I do know what he means, though. Several hours into a run things do get narrowed down until you're alert only to keeping moving. 'Exactly,' he says. 'Eventually it just becomes a game of "What do I need?" And all of a sudden nothing else matters, does it? It's one of the most beautiful moments, standing on the start line of a big challenge. Say the Lakes 24-hour record. I can just push everything else to the side and say, "Right, all I have to do is run and eat and drink, for 24 hours." That's the only thing you have to worry about – and try to enjoy that as much as you can.'

As we talk, it becomes clear that Andy has reconsidered his priorities in light of the value he places on these moments. He works as a plumber subcontracting work from a firm who win contracts from big construction companies and does zero-hours contracts voluntarily. 'Zero-hours contracts work both ways,' he says. 'They don't guarantee me work, but I don't guarantee them that I'll be there. So if I want to go for a run on a Wednesday morning I just go for a run on a Wednesday morning. I can afford that. That's alright.'

'So it's like a different calculation of the value of things,' I suggest. 'Absolutely,' he replies. 'I know how much money I have to earn each week in order to pay the bills and have a little bit left over, and once I hit that sometimes I'll stay a bit longer if I think work will dry up in a few weeks, but other than that I'm going *running*.' He bursts out laughing. When he says he's going running he doesn't mean a couple of hours in Hamsterley, he means he's bundling the dogs into his van and heading for the hills. He just got back from Torridon a couple of days ago.

We begin a long, single-track descent, following a narrow path carpeted with pine needles. As we run, Andy gradually speeds up, nimbly avoiding tree roots as the dogs scamper around us. And as he speeds up, he tells me how central running has become to his identity, the words seeming to spool out faster with his downhill momentum. 'Running was quite a big conflict point in my marriage that didn't work,' he says, 'so coming out of that in 2019 it was a big thing asking myself what I would do. If running had cost me that much, was it really worth it?'

He's flying down the hill at this point and one of the dogs is between the two of us, so I try to keep up whilst also holding my iPhone out in front of me, hoping it is catching what he is saying over the sound of my breathing. He tells me that he was really questioning whether or not he wanted to continue running until he went to support a friend's Bob Graham Round. This is a big run – 66 miles and 42 peaks in 24 hours in the Lake District – and as with other comparable events most people have a relay of 'support' runners, who help by carrying food and water, and often help navigate. 'It was just a beautiful day,' says Andy, 'and we got to the end, and his dream finish was doing it in under 19 hours and we got there with four minutes to spare. And the enjoyment of being part of that, I thought nothing that feels this good can be a negative in my life. So from there I never looked back from that feeling. As long as I can pay the bills and I'm a good dad to James, and I'm there for him, then that's OK.'

From that point on he changed the way his running fitted in with the rest of his life. 'Rather than hiding away my running and waiting until he goes to bed and then getting my run done, I talked to him about it. I explained to him what passion is, what the feeling is around it. Because if you can find your passion, then that's the best gift I could give him.' So they go mountain biking and they're ticking off the Wainwrights together. If he wants to go climbing or paddle boarding they'll do that.

We get to the bottom of the slope and Andy has to wait for me to tentatively negotiate the last little bit, which is strewn with large rocks and tree roots. I apologise when I catch up. 'You have to lift your head up,' he says, 'so that you're looking about 5m away. Your brain is an amazing thing and even if you're looking ahead it will still get your feet to dodge what's right underneath you. It can read the ground.' I like this idea – that you're constantly projecting 5m ahead of you, living a second or so in the future. It's hard to develop that trust in your feet, but I make a mental note to work on it.

To live in Durham whilst longing to be running up and down mountains requires another act of living for the future, one that is a lot less fun than running down a trail in Hamsterley. After Andy has outlined his training to me I say, 'So it sounds like I should try to get on a treadmill a few times before Lakes in a Day?' 'Yeah, I would,' he says. It seems a shame to me that to be able to do the really fun off-road stuff means spending time running indoors and I point this out. 'Well, I just see it as a tool,' he says. 'I love being able to run in those places, so when I get there I want to be able to go as far and as extreme as I can, and get over as many as I can. But it does mean that I have to pick things that really catch my heart, because to prepare for something like the Lakeland 100 in Durham you've got to really fucking want to do it.'

You can't replicate the long climbs of a race in the mountains in Durham, even if you run up and down a hill for hours at a time, because you'll always be able to recover on the downhills. 'You can keep it simple,' he says. 'You could just start with a vertical kilometre, which is 6.8km at 15% incline. It takes between 30 and 40 minutes.' Oh, OK, I think. A nice easy place to start.

'Are there any other ideas I could try?' I ask later on in the run, keen for as many kernels of mountain running wisdom as he is willing to share.

'As long as it's for you and not for the book,' he says, which surprises me. He explains, 'I mentioned a session I do on a podcast and it was like, "Oh, everyone MUST start doing this one thing." You know, the quick-fix problem.'

I could actually benefit from a quick fix of some kind, having left it a bit late to start seriously training for Lakes in a Day, but on principal I completely agree with him. He has recently started coaching online and finds himself having to battle against this kind of mentality, which he thinks is exacerbated massively by platforms like Instagram. 'I think on Instagram it's all "Oh my God, I did this! Look at me everybody!"' and we get lost in making sure we appear successful, and in looking for training hacks. Like, "Do this one session a week and you'll run like Killian [Jornet]." No, you won't!'

This was actually one of the things that frustrated me about going on podcasts to talk about my book about Ethiopian running culture. I was often asked to reduce everything I'd seen and learnt to 'three key takeaways' or one training session that would make you run like the Ethiopians. Even reviews of the book talked about the 'simplicity' of the approach in Ethiopia, which is the opposite of what I'd been trying to communicate: training effectively meant a reorientation of people's entire lives, a series of extremely complex calculations and a whole load of relationships with people who could help you succeed. I explain this to Andy, ending by pointing out that perhaps the most important 'takeaway' was patience, something that is very difficult to market in a sexy way. 'Exactly!' he says.

Even so, a couple of days after meeting him, I am half an hour into an uphill training session on the treadmill in the Durham University gym. I will keep my word to Andy and spare you the details of these treadmill sessions. Frankly, you don't want to know. I am getting funny looks, either because of the small puddle of sweat that is forming on the floor behind the treadmill or because I keep cursing Andy under my breath. He's right, you do have to *really* want to do this, when the reward for watching those metres of ascent creep upwards is not an expanded view, but merely the fact that you are slightly closer to being able to get the hell out of there. I try to remind myself that this will be worth it if it means I'm able to actually run over all those hills in a few weeks' time, like I'm investing in the possibility of some kind of transcendent experience.

I am able to spend some time in the Lake District as well and I go down to meet Jacob Adkin, who moved there from Edinburgh to be in the hills. This time it is a white transit van that I'm looking for, following directions to a pin dropped just off the A66 and sent to me via WhatsApp. We run over Low Rigg and High Rigg in a loop he follows regularly, and he moves up the inclines with unusually short, quick steps, often running with a cadence of 190 steps per minute. This sometimes gives the appearance that he's running over hot coals, but he does so incredibly effectively. In 2019, he won the European Mountain Running Championships in Zermatt, Switzerland.

He is telling me about the injury he suffered recently whilst in the lead of the Home Countries International hill race. 'I was coming down a hill pretty fast, and I put my foot in a bit of a divot and I heard a couple of distinct crunches,' he says. 'So I kind of hopped about a bit and swore a bit. And I gave it a bit of a prod and couldn't really tell how bad it was.'

'Because it was still attached, you mean?' I ask, wondering what he could have learnt from prodding it.

'Exactly. And it was a team competition,' he says. 'I actually went up the next hill about as well as I've ever gone up a hill, with all the adrenaline and frustration, and I still finished fourth.'

He got an x-ray afterwards which showed the bone fragments that had detached themselves from his foot, and then an MRI scan which showed the ligament damage that had literally pulled the bone away. It seems safe to say, then, that it helps to have a high pain threshold for this kind of running.

As we reach the summit of High Rigg we are briefly exposed to a fierce wall of wind that whips across Thirlmere, swallowing our words and allowing me to concentrate on staying upright on the descent. Luckily Jacob is content to run relatively slowly down the rocky slope and I tell him I'm grateful that he's taking it easy. 'I usually run like this in training,' he says. 'But racing is different, especially if you've got people around you. Your brain just clicks off in terms of common sense and you go quicker than you thought was possible.'

He talks about descending in a very similar way to Andy. 'You're thinking five-plus steps ahead,' he says, making scampering down the mountainside sound like a game of chess. 'If you really think about it, it's kind of scary, because you're not thinking about where your feet are now. But once you get better at that kind of technical descent you get to the point where you don't have to think about your feet at all; it's like they're communicating with the ground itself almost. You're connected in a weird way.' He acknowledges that there is something of the cliché to the idea of feeling 'at one' with the fells, but he does believe that this kind of running is doing something that running on the roads does not.

His thoughts on this are also quite similar to Andy's. 'For me it's the sense of freedom that you get from not being on a man-made thing like a road; the ability to explore outside of normal society and the constraints of that. It takes you back to what humans are supposed to be for, just roaming around and enjoying life basically.' I'm surprised by how often he pauses to take in our surroundings as we're running. He stands at the top of a stile and points out the rainbow that has appeared behind us, and at the top of Low Rigg he takes his time orienting me to all the peaks we can see.

'Being on the fells completely disconnects you from any stress,' he goes on. 'Anything on the news, from your life at home or whatever. If you're running on the roads its almost one-dimensional, so your mind does wander to the other stuff. It's only when you've been back at home for a few hours that you realise how much a fell run has detoxified you,' he says. 'It takes a long time for those stresses to come back and seem important again. And you've got more clarity to face them with because of what's just happened on the fells.'

When we hit the road at the end of the run I feel my legs relaxing back into their usual loping cadence after the fells. 'This feels a bit more familiar,' I observe. Jacob, however, is grimacing. 'This is horrible for me,' he says. 'I can't deal with running on the roads much at all.' It is crazy if you think about it that running on the road feels more 'natural' to me than the fells. I wonder if I'll be able to reprogramme myself in time for the race.

* * *

In the race car park in Caldbeck the runners in the van next to mine are enjoying jovially letting me know what I've got myself in for. 'How many times was I sick last year?' one asks, laughing.

'Oh about 19, I think,' comes the response.

'It wasn't, it was only seven or eight! I think lying in the road just shy of here was the funniest bit, wasn't it? Because to your credit you didn't say a word, you just fiddled with your watch and looked the other way.'

It seems clear from talking to them that moments of suffering like this are to be met with laughter rather than sympathy or cajoling: they are very much part of the point of it all. 'One thing you can say for ultra-running,' says one, 'is it takes you to some pretty grim places.'

'Literally, you mean? Or mentally?' I ask.

'Oh, both!' he says enthusiastically, looking out at the rain. I ask what it was that got him started in ultra-running and he laughs. 'You hit 40 and you either buy a soft top car, have an affair with an inappropriate colleague or start running ultras,' he says. 'And we chose wrong.'

They are both inclined to laugh off the question of why so many people are drawn to these events, to revel in their absurdity. After a thoughtful silence, though, one adds, 'If you're slow enough I find it very interesting watching the sun go down on one side of the world and watching it come back up again on the other. That's quite special.'

Perhaps it's not quite the same, but one of the things I find compelling about this race is the idea of starting at dawn and seeing how much of the Lake District I can cover before the sun sets again. It rains persistently throughout the night and I drift in and out of sleep, roused repeatedly by acorns pinging off the roof of the van. I'm relieved when my alarm goes off at 4.45 a.m., keen to get moving. The bus journey to the start reminds me of mornings in Ethiopia, when we would set off at 5 a.m. to arrive at dawn. People snooze around me, and the darkness gradually gives way to blue-grey dawn and green fields. The sheep are plumper than in Ethiopia, though; the grass a deeper green. I hear snippets of conversation as I doze – a pilot and an ICU doctor agree that night shifts are good preparation for ultra-running, whilst someone else talks enthusiastically about a trip to the Galapagos Islands.

Others discuss the route. 'I've been up Helvellyn 12 times this year and only seen the view once,' says one man cheerfully. The visibility today is forecast to be next to nothing. When we get to the start I'm surprised to find I don't feel nervous. It's like my body knows that it needs to save every ounce of energy today. The race organiser tells us that they will almost certainly have to divert the race away from the river crossing, because it has rained so hard it would be unsafe. 'We want you to be able to run the whole course, though,' he says, 'so we'll make that decision as late as we possibly can, when the first runners come down the hill to the river.'

I set off not knowing whether I hope we'll be able to do the crossing or not, and settle into a gentle run out of the village and up the first hill. I really enjoy the early climbing, which was aptly described to me last night as 'yomping through grass', and we make our way in and out of the mist as we head up to High Pike. I fall in step with an enthusiastic, moustachioed runner and we chat away

117

happily for a while. I tell him I'm writing a book about endurance and I'm curious about why so many people are drawn to ultra-running. 'I think we're too comfortable a lot of the time,' he says, echoing what many others have told me. 'We're not designed to be stuck behind a desk. We need to be out having adventures.'

Too many people, he says, end up just coasting through life. 'I don't want to coast through life,' he shouts through the wind. 'I want to gallop through life!' he adds, laughing, before telling me that he twisted his ankle so badly the previous weekend that it was Wednesday before he was walking again. 'I've taken some painkillers already and it's strapped up, so we'll see how we go,' he adds, cheerfully. We lose each other in the mist on the way up, but sure enough he comes – true to his word – galloping past me on the descent to the river crossing, as do a fair few others. I find the descents difficult still, and struggle to trust myself to let go and 'flow' down the steep slopes.

It occurs to me – as it has at several points in this project – that I could have just interviewed people about running the length of the Lake District rather than doing it myself. Anthropologists call the way we do research 'participant observation'. We try to understand social phenomena through careful observation and involvement, without making assumptions. According to anthropologist Tim Ingold, participation requires us to become 'immersed with the whole of our being in the currents of a world-in-formation: in the sunlight we see in, the rain we hear in and the wind we feel in.' Participation isn't opposed to observation, but 'is a condition for it, just as light is a condition for seeing things, sound for hearing them and feeling for touching them.'

This is brilliantly put, I think, and as I reach the bottom of the slippery grass slope I realise that on this occasion my 'immersion' will be quite literal. There are three people braced in the river holding an orange rope against the current to help runners through the fast-flowing water. Just before we get there a final runner passes me, before immediately falling headfirst into the grassy ditch before the river. The guys holding the rope all cheer loudly as he jumps up as if nothing has happened. The water is fast-flowing, but actually quite refreshing and our feet are already so wet from the 'yomping' that it doesn't really matter.

When I speak to the race organiser, Paul, after the race, he talks at length about the delicate balance between giving people a sense of risk and adventure, and keeping them safe. 'We all stand on the start line,' he says, 'you on one side and the race organisers on the other, and none of us really knows how today is going to pan out. It's a world away from a mass participation event.' His task as a race organiser is, in a sense, to cultivate this uncertainty and to facilitate a feeling of adventure. I ask why he thinks this is something that a growing number of people seem to crave. 'I think there's a desire to step outside the structure of modern life,' is how he puts it. 'To do something that isn't structured and where the outcomes are not given, where there's enough unpredictability that you need to be self-reliant.'

The notion of risk is clearly important to Paul. 'A bit of risk is what gets me out of bed in the morning,' he says, 'and I know I'm not alone in that.' But to a certain extent the risk is illusory. They have detailed contingency plans for all kinds of situations, with designated 'places of safety' that they can direct runners to in the case of particularly extreme weather and coaches that sit at various point along the route that would allow them to evacuate the race. They've never had to use them, he says, but they are there for the day when they will. The route itself was designed to be a journey through the wide variety of terrain that the Lake District has to offer, from the high fell to the lakeside calm, with sections of open route choice (where you can choose your own line across the fells as long as you go to the top of certain peaks) and sections on single-track footpaths. The point-to-point course makes it a nightmare for organisers logistically, but it's worth it.

Another way in which Paul seeks to preserve a sense of adventure is through insisting that in order to participate people must be able to navigate, something he sees as a dying art. That's why they deliberately have sections of open route choice and why the route is unmarked on the fells. They do provide a GPX file of the route, but it is deliberately simplified, using straight lines between points on the course. 'We get a depressing number of enquiries saying, "This can't be right – it can't possibly be a straight line over that terrain," he says. 'And we're like, "Yeah, you're supposed to navigate yourself."' There is an interesting paradox here given how many people I talk to about races like this emphasise wanting to escape from technology and experience self-reliance in the hills. In reality, 'a lot of people actually just want to follow an arrow' is how Paul puts it.

Because of the size of the field, and the ebb and flow of pace, I am able to talk to a lot of runners about why they run races like this. Most people mention 'comfort' and a desire to step outside it for a weekend. 'I just think it's an amazing way to spend a day,' is how one puts it. 'I find myself smiling even when it's absolutely miserable.' We are back in the mist again, heading over Mungrisdale Common towards Blencathra, the wind whipping across us in gusts that will peak later at 80mph. I'm soaked to the waist from the river, already muddy and coated in fine droplets of water that mingle with my sweat.

Others talk about events like this as 'adventures' rather than races, opportunities to get lost and found again, to embrace vulnerability and emerge the other side changed in some way, or at least refreshed. The great Czech runner Emil Zatopek once said, 'If you want to run a race, run 100m. If you want to experience a different life, run a marathon.' I'm not sure what he'd have made of ultras, but what a lot of people seemed to be saying is that the appeal lies in experiencing the full gamut of emotional states in the course of a day or more of running.

When I speak to record-breaking ultra-runner Damian Hall a few weeks after my race, he refers to races like the Spine Race (268 miles along the Pennine Way) as 'little holiday-experiments' where he is guaranteed to 'get this rollercoaster of emotions, and there's going to be some doubt and disappointment, and I'm going to get annoyed with myself and frustrated, but there'll definitely also be moments of euphoria.' He describes himself as a 'classically polite and apologetic' British man most of the time, whilst running ultra-marathons allows him to 'peel back the layers of the onion' to a more raw and authentic – and less polite – version of himself.

In one of the increasingly odd voice notes I make to myself in the course of the race I find myself agreeing with him. 'You feel like a petulant child some of the time, like an old man most of the time – it's definitely a way of packing a whole lot of life into a day,' I say, breathlessly. The idea that this is a controlled environment in which to experience vulnerability is one that several people talk to me about. It is interesting that it takes running an ultra-marathon for people to feel that they can admit vulnerability.

Jasmin Paris, who won the women's race (and finished fifth overall) at Lakes in a Day 2022, and more recently became the first female finisher at the notorious Barkley Marathons, also sees ultra-distance events as a way of stepping outside of normal life and providing a fresh perspective. When I speak to her she talks about them as a way to avoid just 'drifting through your existence with nothing really standing out'; as a way of pulling ourselves out of our routine. She talks about going into work on a Monday morning after something like Lakes in a Day or a Mountain Marathon. 'People will talk about having a quiet weekend or maybe watching a bit of telly,' she says. 'And I'm like you have no idea what living is like…'

I find myself wondering how this relates to ideas about 'resilience'. I struggle with this concept, because it is often applauded and seen as something we should all work on, but it also pushes the responsibility for coping on to individuals, and away from institutions and social support networks. Are we embracing vulnerability only to prove that we can find the strength to overcome it or is something more transformative going on?

When we descend out of the wind into Threlkeld it already feels like we've been running for quite a long time. 'It's amazing isn't it, once you get down here you couldn't possibly believe what it's like on the tops,' says one runner cheerfully when we arrive at the aid station, mud splattered all down one side. 'Well, you're about to head straight back up there,' says one of the volunteers, handing him a pastry.

The next leg is the longest and contains most of the hills – Clough Head, The Dodds, Helvellyn and Fairfield – so we stay up in the howling wind and swirling mist for a really long time. Clough Head is a particularly tough climb and is usually the point in the race when people realise exactly what they've got themselves into. As Paul puts it, 'It's an adventure, but it's attritional. And people usually realise that around Clough Head. They go, "Bloody hell, we're going up there! And we've already done one big section of fell!" They realise they've only just scratched the surface of the race and they're already sore, and they realise they have to start thinking about how to manage themselves.'

It's about this point that for most people the notion of doing the race in a particular time or achieving a certain position goes out of the window and it's amazing how accurately this mirrors my experience. On the tops figures appear suddenly out of the mist, sometimes from unexpected directions, looking at watches or maps before dashing off again. On a couple of occasions I try to follow people who seem to know where they're going, but keep losing them when the descents get too technical.

When we picture the Lake District we tend to do so in static ways – we think of picture postcard views or the Romantic tradition of focusing on the aesthetic qualities of the landscape. Here, though, all is movement and we are buffeted this way and that, disorientated and overwhelmed by the noise of the wind. Again, Tim Ingold makes a nice point that the very 'scape' in the word landscape has changed over the centuries. We think of it now as coming from the Greek *skopos* to look, when its etymology can actually be traced to the old English *sceppan* which means 'to shape'. To move through these places, then, is both to shape and be shaped by them.

In this particular case it certainly feels like that; like the wind and the fatigue combine to reduce the separation between the runner and the mountain. I try to let myself go a little more on the descents and to allow the wind to push me this way and that. Whilst in the first 20km or so I was still conscious of being in a race, unable to let go of the habit of working out how many people were in front of me, that has gone now. The sections of open route choice have combined with the thick mist to an extent that I genuinely have no idea where I'm placed in the race, but I also find that I don't care. If it takes me a couple more hours than I'd expected, I decide, it's just more to experience. I might as well make the most of my 'holiday-experiment' and begin to embrace the idea that I might be doing several hours of running in the dark later.

Anthropologists and sociologists who study sport are often concerned with where each example fits on a spectrum between work and play. Scholars in the Marxist tradition, for example, will tend to point to the fact that interval training methods were developed around the same time as 'scientific management' practices and the division of labour were introduced into factory work by people like Frederick Winslow Taylor. Bero Rigauer, for instance, in a book entitled *Sport and Work*, describes the 'repetitive division of the tasks of training and the law of psycho-physical loading' as being directly 'copied from the methods of industrial labour.' Modern sport isn't, therefore, a playful alternative to the world of work, but rather its mirror image – a capitalist corruption of play.

In his classic study, *Man, Play and Games*, Roger Caillois argues that whilst sports require competition (*agôn*) they do not encourage the altering of perceptions (*ilinx*) or leave much room for the imagination. I would agree with the sociologist Michael Atkinson, though, who argues that people embrace sports like fell running because it offers precisely these things. As he puts it, people seek 'the wilful abandonment of personal control and the deliberate embrace of doubt, uncertainty, thrills and anxiety' or what Caillois himself called 'voluptuous panic'.

From the many conversations I have with ultra-runners it certainly seems like this altering of perception is important and not seen as bounded by the activity itself, but rather a lens through which to reflect on the rest of life. It offers a controlled way of letting go of your emotions; a way of stripping things back to the essential task of just moving forward. As I continue running, the hip flexor injury I've been managing for the last few weeks gradually gets worse, so that I'm running quite awkwardly and keep tripping over rocks. I find myself saying things like, 'Ouch' and 'Oh well' out loud when I stub my toe or my foot disappears into a bog – the filter for these kinds of things seems to melt away.

After Ambleside the route is a lot flatter, with stretches along the banks of Lake Windermere. I am tired now and happy to move along at a slower pace. After the tumult of the hill tops a calmness settles over me. It feels like an immense privilege to spend a day doing nothing but running, from first light to well past sundown, and the dramatic changes in both weather and mood make it feel like far longer has passed. As with my cycling experience in Scotland I know that when I get to work on Monday it will feel like more than a weekend separates me from the previous week.

I had been warned that it might be 'a bit wet' along the shore of Lake Windermere, but I am clearly not as used to the understatement of ultra-runners as I thought I was. Several kilometres of the lakeside path are under two feet of cold, muddy water and wading through this is extremely slow going. Sections of the path have a wooden boardwalk raised about a foot off the ground, but this is so submerged in water and weeds that it is very difficult to see, so I am constantly slipping or banging my shins. By the time I finally get to the end my feet and legs are freezing, and I'm not sure I'm going to be able to get them warm again.

I start to jog gingerly again as night falls and I head through several sections of damp forest on leafy trails. Any slight incline forces me into a walk now, but I'm past caring about that. My attention now is occupied only by keeping an eye out for the luminous way markers or following the bobbing headlights of the runners ahead of me. I'm very tired now, over 70km into the race, but keen to see if I can run or at least jog all of the flat sections to the finish. I've already come about 10km further than the furthest I've ever been on foot before and I'm keen to test the limits of my ability to keep running.

The guys in the van next to mine last night had led me to believe the section following the final checkpoint was more or less flat and mostly on the road. I ask one of the volunteers in the aid station about this and he laughs. 'Yeah it's all flat,' he says, 'apart from the uphill bits.' There is indeed still a lot of climbing through forests and running across dark, open fell to negotiate.

I come across the runner I spend the last hour with on the way up a steep, muddy climb. The path is strewn with rocks and fallen branches, and overgrown with brambles. He has poles, but he keeps slipping back down the slope. 'Oh, for goodness sake,' he mutters. Clearly I'm not the only one who voices these matter-of-fact disappointments. Together we make our slow way up the slope and across the fields. Neither of us really has the energy to talk anymore, except to say things like, 'I'm really ready for this to be over now,' but his presence beside me is comforting.

The last couple of miles are on the road – by far the longest stretch of road in the whole race – and it feels good to not have to worry about my footing. We have to run past the racecourse where my van is parked and then through the town where people are watching the rugby in bars or sitting outside with a drink on a balmy October evening. There is definitely some bemusement on the faces of those who watch us struggle past, but we get the odd shout of encouragement too. I cross the line with my companion and we congratulate each other before collapsing into chairs by the finish. I know it's going to be a real struggle to get up again.

Finally I get myself into a hot shower. I could stay there all night, letting the water ease my aching muscles, but I want to be at the finish line. Remarkably, at 10 p.m. in October, it is still warm enough to sit on the ground with a cold can of Fell Runner ale and watch people arrive. I feel an amazing sense of calm and time slips away with me sitting there chatting to whoever gingerly lowers themselves to the ground next to me. Before I know it, it's almost midnight and I'm not sure I can trust my legs to get me back upright.

Every few minutes a new arrival is heralded by the appearance of a bobbing head torch beam over the wall to my right, before they turn the corner and break into a smile or hold their arms aloft. A lot of people arrive in pairs, like I did, or groups of three or even four. 'Oh mate, thank you,' one man says, as he wraps his arms around his companion in a muddy, sweaty embrace, before adding, 'Nice to meet you.' This sums up the interactions perfectly. There is an intimacy to them that makes you think people have known each other for years, when in reality they met an hour and a half ago in a dark field and decided to go onwards together.

'It's incredible the bond you can create with someone over 20km of an ultra,' is how one guy who sits down with me puts it. 'There are people I met that way years ago who I'm still in touch with.' I sit on the floor in awe of the people coming in, but also asking myself what it all means. Running something like this is in many ways an extravagantly excessive use of energy and it is no surprise that the participants are almost entirely white, or that the vast majority are middle class, or that there are more than three times as many men as there are women, who tend to be given a harder time when justifying spending their weekends away from their kids running around the fells.

It does seem clear, though, that the number of people wanting to experience these kinds of events is growing exponentially and that they are gradually becoming more diverse and inclusive. It seems clear from the many conversations I've had with people that pushing their limits in this way involves some kind of critical reflection on the world or the way we live within it. The sociologist Stephen Lyng borrows the term 'edgework' from the gonzo journalist Hunter S Thompson to describe these kinds of activities that push people towards some kind of limit.

'To conceive of this kind of behaviour as edgework,' he writes, 'is to understand it as a type of experiential anarchy in which the individual moves beyond the realm of established social patterns to the very fringes of ordered reality.' For him, the fact that so many people find this sort of thing compelling 'is an important critical statement on the nature of modern social life.' People gain a sense of control and mastery from getting close to the edge without quite going over it, and this extends to other aspects of their lives.

Edgework activities provide an escape from the routine and predictable, the excessive 'comfort' many people mentioned on the run. For Damian Hall, they also represent a reaction to 'peak consumerism or peak big technology', although he acknowledges that they are often intertwined, with people using social media to tell their stories and expensive GPS watches to navigate. 'My phone gets turned off at the beginning of an event,' he says, 'and you sort of realise I don't need my phone, I don't need to check my emails,' which are things he finds himself addicted to most of the time.

The kind of events that Damian does, which involve running for three days and nights, are perhaps an extreme way of battling phone addiction, but it does seem that the people who take part in them, and shorter races like Lakes in a Day, crave a kind of simplicity that is often hard to find. However, these experiences also allow us to acknowledge that life is full of risks and uncertainty, and give us an opportunity to confront these kinds of risks head on within a controlled environment. It is unsurprising, then, that so many people took to these endurance challenges during and after the uncertainty and flux of the Covid-19 pandemic.

Many of those I talked to as I ran from Caldbeck to Cartmel reflected on how 'amazing' the human body is and how important it is to take opportunities to remind ourselves of this. It is quite remarkable that most people, even if they have to go slowly, can keep going for a whole day and most of a night. This kind of statement is almost always followed by another, which is that doing an event like this is at least 50% about the power of the mind and that the further you go the more important the mental aspect becomes.

When pedestrianism was the most-watched sport in the world, it was because people were fascinated by this kind of human ability in the face of creeping automation and particularly the introduction of motorised vehicles, which meant it was no longer necessary for many to walk long distances. As I sit on the ground watching people stagger towards the finish line I wonder if what we are seeing is a similar reaction to worries about the introduction of AI and the increasing spread of automation. Running all day is a way of screaming out that we are still uniquely human; that there are things that we can do and experience that can't be replaced by new technology.

The protagonist of Kurt Vonnegut's first novel, *Player Piano*, driven to distraction by the replacement of human workers by machines, says, 'I want to stand as close to the edge as I can without going over. Out on the edge you can see all kinds of things you can't see from the centre.' It is tempting to perceive something of this perspective in ultra-running – we look for the edge in order to reflect on what is happening in the world from a new vantage point.

6

TECHNOLOGY AND THE ELEPHANT IN THE ROOM

My friend Jemal Yimer, who is the former Ethiopian record holder in the half marathon and still one of the fastest runners in history with a best time of 58.33, has frequent blood tests at his home in Ethiopia. Because he is in the World Athletics Registered Testing Pool he is required to update an online system with his 'whereabouts' at all times, so that the drug testers can find him during a one-hour period each day to take a blood sample, something that makes it very difficult for athletes to make spontaneous decisions about visiting family or altering their training sessions. This is also not that easy in Addis Ababa, where there are no street names and addresses are more likely to be given as vague descriptions in relation to a local landmark.

The 'whereabouts' system also isn't available in Amharic, which makes it difficult to navigate for athletes who don't read English or who are less familiar with technology. What this means in practice is that a system that should be confidential actually requires a complex series of communications between the athlete and their sub-agent in Ethiopia, who communicates with their manager (usually in Europe), who eventually updates the system, which is supposed to be completed three months in advance. In spite of this, the World Anti-Doping Agency (WADA) rules state that athletes are solely responsible for providing information and 'cannot blame their representative or agent for inaccurately filing or forgetting to update their whereabouts information.'

The new system for drug-testing elite athletes is called the Athlete Biological Passport (ABP). Because it is now possible to produce synthetic performance-enhancing substances like testosterone and erythropoietin (EPO) that are so similar to the naturally produced substances that they are undetectable through conventional testing, the ABP tracks blood values over time, so that officials at the Athletics Integrity Unit (AIU) can scrutinise them for suspicious fluctuations. The chemists who developed the system have noted the interest of pharmaceutical companies who see its potential use for developing personalised medicine in the future, potentially allowing (presumably wealthy) patients to detect illnesses as early as possible and insurance companies to save money.

The *Lancet* has noted that this marks a significant shift. Whilst in the past performance-enhancing drugs were initially developed to address specific medical issues – severe anaemia for patients on kidney dialysis in the case of EPO, for example – what we are now seeing is the development of testing practices for sport going the *other way* and becoming medically useful. The logic of the ABP used for professional athletes – of carefully tracking changes over time – is the same as the logic behind products like Inside Tracker and Forth Edge, which are explicitly marketed as providing performance-enhancing insights to amateur endurance athletes in the UK and US.

Forth Edge claims to 'give you unparalleled insight into how your body works, races and recovers.' Inside Tracker promises to provide a 'path to living healthier longer'. Both present the blood values of recreational athletes who subscribe to them in a visually compelling way via an app. Whether or not you believe that these things actually *do* provide insights which provide a performance advantage, it is striking that the data produced by these two quite similar forms of regular testing are used so differently – in the case of professional athletes like Jemal it is used exclusively to catch them out, whilst for amateurs it is to improve their performance.

In the 2022 Chicago marathon, Jemal was able to run with the lead group for much of the race, but it felt like he was making more effort than normal to stay in touch with the group. Used to finishing on or near the podium in big races like this, he was fighting just to remain in the pack and eventually had to accept that it wasn't going to be his day shortly after the 30km mark. He'd not been feeling quite right in training in the final weeks leading up to the race, but had put this down to the usual marathon fatigue. The competitive moment was where it mattered, though, and as he stepped off the road and on to the pavement he wondered two things: how was he going to get back to the hotel and what was wrong with him?

The Chicago marathon look after their elite athletes well, and he was in the back of a car and on the way back to the race hotel very quickly. The answer to his second question had to wait until he got back to Addis Ababa and was able to see Dr Ayalew at the Ethiopian Athletics Federation. As it turned out, he had been running with clinically low iron levels – it was a miracle he was able to run with the leaders for as long as he did. Jemal was frustrated. If he'd had access to products like Inside Tracker to monitor his iron and haemoglobin levels, he thinks he would have been in a position to win Chicago.

The fact that leading up to the race he *had* actually undergone regular blood testing, as often as twice a week, was especially frustrating. Had these tests been used – as their designers originally intended – to help to monitor and maintain his health as well as ensure he wasn't infringing doping rules, he wouldn't have been in this situation. The data gathered by the Athletics Integrity Unit is collected purely for surveillance purposes, however, and Jemal wasn't told that his iron levels were dangerously low. As Hailye Teshome, the sub-agent who works with him and his manager in Ethiopia, put it, 'There is a huge gap between our athletes and yours' in terms of access to information. Even world-class athletes who make hundreds of thousands of dollars a year do not see sports doctors regularly and there is no specialist sports rehabilitation hospital in the country. It is possible to seek out private medical care for a blood test, but it is not something athletes are encouraged to do.

From Hailye's perspective, European and American athletes are 'far more advanced', an idea that I find interesting given that it is so obviously not the case in terms of the performances athletes are able to produce on the roads. If recreational athletes are at times overcomplicating their training and the monitoring of their bodies through an over-reliance on data, it conversely seems like some of the best athletes in the world would benefit from a little more information in certain situations.

The conversation about global sporting ethics – both in the media and in academia – is entirely dominated by the issue of doping and the presence of particular pharmaceutical substances. The notion of fairness in Ethiopia was quite different, however. When I was at a half marathon race in Hawassa in 2016, for example, I was handed a leaflet about anti-doping that featured a picture of Abebe Bikila and the slogan 'Rome Gold, Tokyo Gold, No Shoes'. It described an idealised notion of sporting purity in which technology – even in the form of footwear – played no part.

It is striking how quickly we have come to accept the clearly performance-enhancing nature of footwear since I was given this flyer. In Ethiopia access to carbon fibre-plated shoes is still limited to those who are sponsored by one of the top brands unless you happen to have $500 to spend on the black market. This has already severely skewed competition at the domestic level, making it difficult for young athletes to break through. Unsure of how to react to the first Nike prototypes featuring a propulsion plate, the shoes were sent to the Ethiopian Athletics Federation's anti-doping office to be dismantled and assessed. The conclusion was that these were clearly dramatically performance enhancing and should be banned (the men's marathon world record has improved by two and a half minutes since their introduction), yet the Ethiopians had no way of influencing regulation of the shoes on the global level.

When asked about what fairness meant to them as athletes, the runners I knew almost always talked about the equal sharing of resources. Tsedat Ayana, for example, who ran his PB of 2.06.18 at the Dubai marathon in 2020, told me, 'Fair sport means when things are distributed equally and will not benefit one party.' For him, the important thing is that all athletes, in regional clubs, at Province level and in first division clubs in the city, 'get equal distribution of services and facilities.' This means they should all have access to a track, to decent running kit, to coaching support and massage therapy, but also to good quality food and a decent place to sleep. It is the equal distribution of opportunity and resources that motivates athletes' behaviour, as well as their attitudes towards doping.

One morning, we drove out to Sendafa to the east of Addis Ababa, parking at the end of a line of Hyundai i10s, the car of choice for the up-and-coming marathon runner. The sub-agent of our group reached into the footwell and retrieved a series of black bin bags containing boxes of pills, each bound with an elastic band. One by one, athletes got into the back seat and were given the boxes, stuffing them furtively to the bottom of their kitbags.

The boxes contained multivitamins produced by a Dutch company called Virtuoos, which markets itself as 'the number one in pure sports supplements'. The vitamins are batch-tested for the absence of prohibited substances, making them significantly more expensive than equivalent vitamins, which means, their maker claims, 'You can order all your supplements from Virtuoos without any worries or hesitation.' The vitamins were ordered by the athletes' manager after a member of the training group found out about them from athletes in another world-class training group in Addis. Before ordering them, he checked that there was absolutely no risk of contamination and that he could be confident that they were 'clean'. Why, then, would athletes feel the need to carefully conceal these especially 'virtuous' vitamins?

The reason is that Amhara long-distance runners believe that success is collectively produced and that energy is a limited substance that has to be shared equally. As I've mentioned, this means that people place a huge amount of emphasis on training together, to the extent that going for a run on your own, and especially doing hard training alone, is seen as deeply anti-social. Training is something that should be synchronous and visible to others, with everyone doing the same thing. Only in this way can energy expenditure be monitored. If you train hard on your own, you damage your ability to help the team.

So taking these vitamins was seen as a selfish 'shortcut' by those who didn't have access to them. The runners I knew were almost all devout Orthodox Christians and the values they spoke about most were patience, consistency and humility, and the acceptance that they needed to work together over a long period of time. A 'shortcut' might be trying to do extra training at night, which was seen as detrimental to your teammates, or it might mean engaging in witchcraft to steal the energy of others. Or it might mean taking vitamins. In all cases, 'shortcuts' were instances of individualistic behaviour, or engaging in things that not everybody was able to do.

Doping was seen as particularly nefarious behaviour, because the vast majority of athletes had no access to performance-enhancing drugs, which were seen as entering the country through exclusive networks and were far too expensive to even be considered by most runners. Taking drugs was seen as a desperate act that would have dire consequences later in life – athletes compared it to a pact with the devil. These consequences varied, but people talked about cancer, about car accidents, about people losing their money and their minds. I therefore find the flippancy with which some people assume that large numbers of athletes in Ethiopia must be doping very frustrating.

It also seems important to think more carefully about what fairness means in endurance sports. In October 2019 a 19-year-old Ethiopian runner and acquaintance of mine was notified by the sub-agent of his training group that he had failed a drugs test at a European half marathon three weeks previously. He was given seven days to provide a written statement (in English) explaining the 'adverse analytic finding'. He could also have his 'B sample' tested (blood samples are split into two portions so one can be retained) and was welcome to attend the laboratory in Europe to witness the test or view the 'laboratory documentation package' supporting it, the costs of which, he was informed, 'shall be borne entirely by you.' Unable to afford these things and in a state of confusion about what exactly he had been charged with and why, he was banned from competition for four years.

In the same month, the Nike Oregon Project in America, which was set up for the explicit reason of 'ending the dominance' of East African athletes, was closed down after head coach Alberto Salazar was banned for 'orchestrating and facilitating doping conduct'. Often in the limelight for pushing boundaries, for instance by issuing 'therapeutic use exemptions' for thyroid medication and L-carnitine infusions or by constructing 'altitude houses', where one or more rooms was sealed and the oxygen levels controlled to mimic being at altitude, no athlete from the project has faced a ban from the sport and Salazar was able to take his appeal to the Court of Arbitration for Sport (CAS) with the financial support of the world's biggest sportswear company, Nike.

CAS upheld the four-year bans imposed on Salazar and Dr Jeffrey Brown who worked with many of the Oregon Project's top athletes. Whilst none of the athletes coached by Salazar failed drugs tests themselves, it seems fairly obvious that there is a huge difference in the capacity of athletes in these two different contexts to negotiate this system, and especially to push boundaries whilst remaining just on the right side of the line between legal and illegal, which seems to define high-performance sports culture in wealthy countries. There are many cases in which medical and scientific knowledge is used to ensure that athletes do not fail drugs tests, whilst also gaining a significant performance advantage.

In spite of this, it is East Africa that is portrayed as the doping 'hotspot' (Martha Kelner in the *Guardian*) for endurance sports, and as a place of 'crisis' (*Athletics Illustrated*) where testing is lax and athletes are more likely to break the rules because of 'relative poverty', as Kelner put it. The way that the ABP is implemented is supposed to resemble a forensic approach to crime fighting, allowing a legal case to be built based on probabilities. What makes it very different from criminal cases, though, is that athletes are not given the usual presumption of innocence.

In a high-profile case that came to light in May 2023, Rhonex Kipruto, the Kenyan world record-holder for 10km, was provisionally suspended from competition for alleged inconsistencies in his ABP dating back to 2018. His management company, Ikaika Sport, issued an impassioned press release protesting against his ban, describing the 'presumption of guilt' as a 'Kafkaesque drama'. Whilst they have consulted with expert biochemists and sports doctors and with a legal team (incurring costs of $30,000) they note the impossibility of countering the claims adequately, because they have not been permitted to access the data on which the decision to ban Kipruto was made.

It is clear from the independent experts they consulted that, as one of them put it, 'There are other plausible explanations of the ABP values other than doping.' These include factors such as training load, health status, hydration status, travel, significant alcohol consumption and how the body reacts under different circumstances. Crucially, they also argue that, 'The ABP model is potentially not accurate with respect to East African athletes, especially in relation to 1% of a 1% when it comes to absolute talent, born and raised in harshest conditions, but still being able to perform at the pinnacle of human ability.'

Indeed, the studies on which the adaptive model is based rely on a small number of Caucasian participants, the majority of whom were amateur rather than elite athletes. Larger studies use the category of 'Africa', an entire continent, and fail to account for the specificities of living and training at altitude, which is one of the main factors in creating variation in blood values. Moreover, as Kipruto's team had no access to the relevant data, and as in general the 'statistical analysis' on which the ABP relies is 'not available to the scientific community' and 'does not follow the classical decision-making approach of medicine and science,' as Giuseppe Banfi, a professor in clinical biochemistry and molecular biology at the University of Milan, puts it in the journal *Clinical Chemistry and Laboratory Medicine*, there is a clear issue of data availability and transparency. As Ikaika Sports says, 'We are not in a position of a level playing field.'

With this idea of fairness, and the notion of opportunities and resources for all, in mind I decide to talk to Aron D'Souza about his vision for an Enhanced Games, which seems explicitly designed to turn the conventional world of sport and our idea of human limits on its head. As far as Aron is concerned, the modern Olympic Games is run primarily in the interests of the International Olympic Committee at the expense of the athletes who actually compete. His solution is twofold: provide far greater financial incentives for athletes and 'openly celebrate science', by allowing the use of performance-enhancing drugs and technologies under carefully controlled circumstances.

Aron is a busy man. He's only a couple of years older than me, but in addition to getting his PhD in legal philosophy he has already had a series of careers, first leading Peter Thiel's litigation against Gawker media, then launching 'a bunch' of fintech companies in Australia. He has given himself little more than two years to raise the investment for his games, refine the concept and do all the practical and logistical work for an event that, at the time of our conversation, has yet to have a publicly announced venue. For comparison, Paris was awarded the 2024 Olympic Games in 2017, with the organising committee already having put together a hugely detailed and fully costed proposal. We therefore have a 'hard stop' on our Zoom call at 30 minutes, and I am relieved to find that he likes to make his points succinctly and forcefully.

He sees the International Olympic Committee as 'probably the most corrupt organisation in the world after FIFA' and believes the Olympic Games require major reform. He thinks the four-year Olympic cycle doesn't work for athletes and is unfit for the 21st century. 'We need to be giving athletes an opportunity to monetise,' is how he puts it. 'We live in a TikTok era.' He wants to create a fairer economic situation for athletes, something that I agree with him is long overdue. To give a sense of the lack of money in athletics, gold medallists at the World Athletics Indoor Championships, which only occur once every two years, won $40,000 for proving themselves to be the absolute best in the world in their event. Cristiano Ronaldo earns this much every hour and a half. 'The Olympics does not salary its athletes,' he goes on. 'Therefore it can only ask certain things of them.'

His vision is to offer athletes generous remuneration, but at a cost. 'To be an enhanced athlete,' he goes on, 'you must wear an Apple Watch. You must give us all that data from your Apple Watch: your sleep cycles, your oximeter, your VO_2. And we can use that data to inform drug discovery, to design the next great products out there, then recycle the profits from those pharmaceutical or lifestyle interventions back towards paying more athletes, getting more data and building the future.'

It is clear from chapter 3 that people seem very happy to give this data away for free and will even pay for the privilege of giving it away, so I agree with him that paying athletes for what is actually very valuable data seems like a good idea. I tell him about athletes like Jemal, who are in the World Athletics Registered Testing Pool and therefore give blood samples regularly, for whom having access to the information would be a good thing. 'Yeah,' he says, 'but athletes aren't going to allow the secret police at WADA to use their biological information and go and build biotechnology tools, because it's this negative relationship.'

This is true, of course. What Aron wants to offer athletes who push the absolute limits of speed and endurance is the chance to be 'remunerated, well treated and contribute to human flourishing through genetic testing, bioinformatics, genomics testing, in a very positive way.' The world's best athletes thus become representatives of human potential, blazing a trail that others can follow.

It seems quite clear to me that this isn't really about sport, so I ask how his project relates to the interest in human enhancement and longevity in Silicon Valley. 'Actually I believe that the efforts of the World Anti-Doping Authority and the national anti-doping commissions hold back human progress,' he says, 'because sport is the most obvious way that we should be illustrating the efficacy of anti-ageing or performance medicine technologies.' One of his key objectives, in fact, is to 'defund' anti-doping organisations. Aron has had a 20-year career in venture capital, including experience of running his own funds, but even he was surprised by how easy it was to raise money. 'We've signed with some of the biggest venture capital funds in Silicon Valley,' he says. 'We expect to raise hundreds of millions of dollars over the next few years to build this into a reality, not just in terms of the games, but also the biotechnology and R&D side.'

The attraction of the games for pharmaceutical and biotechnology companies is obvious. Aron imagines a scenario like this: 'Oh look, we took the 100m world record from 9.5 to 8.9 seconds, obliterated it overnight, and the first thing everybody's going to say is, "What was that guy on and how do I get it?"' Admittedly it does seem likely that would be the case and it seems like a large part of the motivation here is to normalise the use of these kinds of enhancements and then see them gradually be adopted by the general public, but my concern is what kind of effect this would have on society more widely. 'How do you think this relates to the world of work more generally?' I ask. 'If you're speeding up how fast people can run, how far they can throw things, will there be knock-on effects for the rest of the economy in terms of speeding everything up?'

He is unequivocal about this. 'Oh absolutely. Absolutely. The way I think of this is that it's like Formula One. McLaren and Ferrari spend millions developing the latest carbon ceramic brakes and then that technology diffuses out to their race cars, then their road cars and then to the everyday Honda Civic on the street. And you know, in a very similar way we can use track and field, swimming and other sports to illustrate the efficacy and the safety of enhancements.' The overall effect of this, he says, will be that, 'As a population we will be younger, faster, stronger and thinner for longer.'

He is convinced that this is the next big industry and that it's one that Britain should be spearheading. This was the focus of the speech he gave at the First Conference on Human Enhancement, held in early 2024 at the House of Lords. In a room with everyone from venture capitalists to the founder of the Rejuvenation Olympics, and experts on ageing, cardiology and performance-enhancing drugs (and one anthropologist), his speech focused primarily on this aspect of his project. He lists a range of industries, from glass and telecommunications to the internet and artificial intelligence, in which Britain pioneered the early research only to miss out on most of the profits.

Clearly there are many people who would want to be younger, faster and thinner, but the assumption that this would work for the whole 'population' reminds me of the fantasy of trickle-down economics and I find myself asking whether this is just another way for the top 1% of society to separate themselves from everyone else. I also wonder what the effect of normalising enhancement technologies in the workplace would be. Drugs that improve alertness or cognitive functioning would clearly boost productivity in some industries – they already do so in finance, and in the military – and if this were normalised to the extent that it became expected, it would reconfigure our understanding of normal human physical and mental limits. Perhaps, then, this would allow us to work more efficiently and free up more time for the things we really value – like running ultra-marathons!

People have been hoping that new technologies and increasing automation would free up time for people to do the things they truly value for decades, but in fact many of us feel like there has been an intensification in our working hours and an expectation that we work harder and for longer. The reaction to the announcement of the Enhanced Games has ranged from mockery to outrage, with very few openly supporting it. Aron thinks the pushback is fading away, though, citing statistics about the high percentage of men who use gyms expressing an interest in anabolic steroids. What I find most interesting about this is that we so openly embrace wearable technologies, willingly giving our bodily data away for free in the name of performance enhancement, and yet we reject what Aron is doing in such strong terms. It seems to me that the logic of this aspect of the project at least is not really that different.

So what about technology? If endurance sport is about pushing our limits and learning something along the way, do things like the new generation of 'super shoes' augment or diminish this? In a history of sporting culture that ranges from Athens to the Apaches and Aztecs, the historian Allen Guttmann argues that sport has gradually transformed from having ritual qualities towards being primarily about the worship of the record. As he puts it, 'Once the Gods have vanished from Mount Olympus or from Dante's paradise, we can no longer run to appease them or to save our souls, but we can set a new record. It is a uniquely modern form of immortality.'

As sports modernised, they came to emphasise the importance of institutionalisation, rationalisation and, crucially, comparison between countries and eras. The record was a 'marvellous abstraction' that allowed for comparisons to be made not only between those gathered at a particular event, but amongst everyone who had ever competed all around the world. But what happens when a record – which, according to Guttmann, is a form of 'immortality' – is ascribed primarily to a new pharmaceutical discovery or another 'breakthrough' in shoe technology, rather than a human?

This was, it should be noted, a concern of Pierre de Coubertin, the founder of the modern Olympics and the man most closely associated with the Olympic 'values' and 'spirit'. In 1936 he foresaw shoes with springs that would 'somehow throw the runner forward with each step', which is a fairly accurate description of the mechanism of recent shoe technology. This would make the effort of running easier, he said, but noted that therefore 'the speed achieved in this way will not be entirely [their] own.'

In autumn 2023 both the women's and men's marathon records were broken in quick succession. The vast majority of the coverage of these records was about the shoes that were worn. When Tigist Assefa ran an astonishing 2.11.53 at the Berlin marathon, the articles about the race included next to no information about who she was or what motivated her to run so fast. The few quotes that did appear were mostly about the shoes she was wearing: a new Adidas model that had to be thrown away after a single use. Two weeks later, when Kelvin Kiptum broke the men's world record in a new Nike shoe, the *Telegraph* article about his run was entitled 'Nike hit back at Adidas in "super shoe" war', a framing of his performance that was echoed in many other publications.

We are still, clearly, in the era of the 'record' as Guttman defines it, but we have moved from worshipping the athlete to worshipping technological innovation, which serves to diminish the achievements of the people involved. It may also quite drastically change which athletes win races and break records, as the latest research on carbon-plated shoes indicates a large amount of variation in the advantage they give particular athletes, depending on the specific combination of runner and shoe technology. As the sports scientist, engineer and international ultra-runner Geoffrey Burns puts it, 'the individual diversity of benefit likely has a greater range than we have seen before.' His responses to my questions are cautious and full of caveats, because many of the studies are narrow in their scope and size and often not particularly well designed (including one that showed a shoe providing anything from an 11% detriment to an 11% improvement in running economy) and because he is sceptical about lab-based results translating perfectly to real-life situations.

Of the better designed studies, the range in improvement in running economy is usually somewhere between 2% and 6%, which is still a significant difference, and greater than the variation between 'old' style racing shoes. It is also unclear from current studies how different people 'adapt' to the shoes, and whether some people are better at making the subtle changes in biomechanics required to make the most of running in them without being injured.

It is likely that we will see the emergence of more custom-made shoes and that more athletes will undergo lab testing to see which brand best suits their own biomechanics, but also that access to this kind of testing will be unevenly distributed. The fact that the coverage of their world records was dominated by discussion of the shoes rather than the athletes themselves is compounded, of course, by the fact that Assefa and Kiptum are from Ethiopia and Kenya – no doubt we would have learned a lot more about them had the athletes in question been white. It is also important to think carefully about where we want this to stop. Who do we want to celebrate through endurance sports, the athletes themselves or pharmaceutical companies and corporations like Nike and Adidas?

7

ENDURING SOCIAL MEDIA

Parker Stinson is running towards us along a deserted country road. Snow falls diagonally from left to right across the scene, so heavily that the trees behind the runner take on a ghostly appearance. The footage cuts to show him in profile, a picket fence flashing past behind him and fields in white-out behind that. His arms drive hard to his chest as he lowers his head to protect his eyes from the snow as a fragment of a Drake rap plays. The caption beneath the video reads, 'Whatever it takes!' followed by a description of Parker's training session that day and the hashtags used by his main sponsors. Responses to the video include comments like, 'Beast' with a flexed bicep emoji and 'Adverse conditions badassery.'

It is, undoubtedly, an inspiring video. It makes you want to get up and run a hard fartlek session like Parker, wishing you could run like he does, with an elastic energy that is somehow at once erratic and silky smooth. The video has over 8000 likes on Instagram, but it will have been viewed many more times and appeared on countless other people's feeds. Few will think for very long about the process by which the video came about or the logistics behind its filming or about why Parker felt compelled to make the video in the first place. However, given that so many recreational endurance athletes use Instagram to tell their own stories, often mimicking the way elite athletes use these platforms, it is interesting to go behind the scenes of these posts to see what this reveals and to help us to think more carefully about our use of social media.

Parker is an American professional marathon runner and the national record holder for 25km. The day we sit down to chat he has had a particularly easy training day – a six-mile run and some stretching – and I can hear the excess energy in his voice when we speak over Zoom. His enthusiasm is infectious and he has the endearing habit of peppering his speech with the name of the person he is talking to. I ask first about the video of him running in the snow. 'Did you think to yourself before the run, "It's going to be snowing – I should get some footage of this?"' I ask.

'That's a great question, Mike,' he says. 'Absolutely, that's exactly how it came about.' He is very keen to emphasise, though, that he didn't 'sit around all day' hoping to run in those conditions, because he had to fit in physio treatment in the morning. He looked up the forecast for the afternoon. 'I thought, this is going to suck,' he says, laughing. 'So I hit up my photographer guy and said, "Are you free? You should come out and get some photos and video. I think this could be pretty cool."' Throughout our conversation he is keen to impress upon me the importance of authenticity on social media. He definitely had an idea of how filming in the snow might look, and co-ordinating a professional photographer to come and shoot it could seem contrived, 'but I didn't change anything,' he emphasises. 'I'm not stopping and doing a stride [running 100m or so quickly as part of a warm-up] to get a shot. I did my workout.'

Scroll though running X or Instagram and you are confronted with a lot of posts like this, either captured by professional photographers and videographers on behalf of professional athletes or by runners themselves, who must set them up in far more convoluted ways. Having spoken to a lot of professional runners about how they manage their social media, I can't help but wonder about the ways in which many of the images that circulate on these platforms are created. Take that 10-second clip of the runner on their favourite section of single-track. How long did it take them to prop their phone at exactly the right angle to capture it? Did they have to make a mad dash in the opposite direction in order to then jog serenely past their phone at the right moment? How many takes did they have to do before they got it right? Did the whole enterprise enhance their experience of their run or was it experienced as an interruption? What, in short, compelled them to do it?

So how does our use of social media change how we think about endurance sport? As with self-tracking technologies, I am not necessarily advocating for everyone to delete their accounts, but we should probably think a bit more carefully about how we use these platforms and why.

I spent parts of the various Covid-19 lockdowns speaking to professional athletes about their use of social media and about how posting regularly and being able to tell a story online has become almost as much of the 'work' of a professional athlete as running or cycling fast or scaling new peaks. As the American marathon runner Noah Droddy put it in a tweet: 'Professional running is 50% posting on social media, 30% training, and 20% explaining to people why you aren't going to the Olympics.' This is clearly tongue-in-cheek, but it actually stands up statistically as the athletes I spoke to reported five or six hours of screen time per day versus two or three of training.

At the professional level, sports like running and climbing are particularly precarious forms of employment, relying heavily on sponsorship related to the sport as opposed to salaries from teams. With the exception of those at the absolute pinnacle of their sports, using social media is an obligation, not a choice. One of the American runners I spoke to compares this to American football players. 'After a bad year, the offensive linemen for one NFL team were getting berated by their fans on social media,' he says, 'so they all just deleted their accounts. It wasn't worth it. But running is a sport where we need it to survive, and we don't have the luxury of just being able to block for our quarterback and still get paid millions. We have to take on that $5000 contract with a supplement company and post three times a month in order to make a living.' He pauses before adding, 'It's a lot of hustling for sure.'

Many athletes spoke of pivoting towards a greater focus on social media because of Covid-19 – a lack of competitive opportunities meant that they had to seek other ways of increasing their income. However, it is also clear that, regardless of the pandemic, sponsorship deals with major brands are now conditional on posting frequently on social media, to the extent that athletes struggle to know whether their job is running fast or creating compelling content, or how these things are balanced against each other. As another athlete puts it, 'Say you've got someone who runs 27.30 [for 10km] with no social media presence versus someone who runs 28.05, but tells his story, humanises the hero, gets people cheering for him in his race. He's going to get a much bigger contract at this point, which is kind of strange.'

For some, this is deeply frustrating and they think athletes' pay should be based entirely on performance. For others, the increasing importance of social media only exaggerates an already existing trend: more charismatic athletes have always been paid more money. What does seem apparent, though, is that the thing most athletes are passionate about is trying to run fast and win races or climb routes that have never before been climbed. They would prefer their worth to their sponsors to be tied to their athletic performances, and experience much of the peripheral labour of posting on social media and creating content as working against those goals.

Athletes are very aware that performance metrics determine their future in the sport – whether they hit the qualifying time for the Olympics, for example, or finish in the top three in their national trials. Today, though, they are becoming reliant upon different kinds of metrics, such as Instagram analytics about engagement with their posts on social media. In this sense they have become a little like workers on platforms like Deliveroo, who are intimately aware that their ability to hit performance metrics shapes their ability to continue working for the platform. The most frustrating thing about this for many athletes is that they are suddenly expected to be able to think like a marketing executive, social media manager or professional photographer, without any training or assistance with any of these roles. For some this comes quite naturally to them, but for others it is experienced as stressful and exhausting. As one of the athletes I speak to puts it, 'I find that it takes something out of me to create that content. It's draining for me in the same way it would be to walk through a room of people and have to talk to everybody.'

Dana Giordano has come back from the track just in time to make some soup and talk to me, and she has so much to say that I keep worrying that her soup is getting cold. I am particularly keen to talk to her because of a tweet of hers that epitomised a shift in the way of thinking about what it means to be a professional endurance athlete. As the first of many race cancellations were announced, she tweeted: 'After a month or so of panic and waiting to hear if the Olympics were postponed, I put my energy into something else. Building my personal brand.'

Endurance athletes are often portrayed as embodying an ascetic existence characterised by withdrawal from society and long periods of time spent training in remote, often mountainous, places or away climbing in inaccessible areas. The word 'sacrifice' is used a lot, and there has always been a certain mystique verging on secrecy to the highland plateaus and snowy altitude retreats people disappear to in order to reach the highest levels. For endurance runners this is particularly true, the 'loneliness of the long-distance runner' being part of that sacrifice they make and the mythology of the sport. Athletes would emerge into the limelight only a few times a year in order to compete, before disappearing once more. In this sense they are something like saints: we are moved by what they are able to do as a result of the lifestyles they pursue, but we do not necessarily want the life of discipline they have chosen.

This has changed dramatically in recent years. Social media has given those following the sport a window into the day-to-day lives of elite endurance athletes, which has shifted the focus away from specific competitive performances towards the ability to craft a compelling narrative about your athletic life. As Dana puts it, a lot of being a professional athlete is about building a personal brand. This means trying to be 'authentic' and working to be as visible as possible by posting with a consistency that gives people a sense of your whole life – Dana Giordano getting a milkshake, Dana Giordano using a foam roller, Dana Giordano going to the physio (again).

'Some days,' she says, 'there's that pressure of "Oh shoot, I haven't posted a photo this week at all!"' She likes to post at least three times a week on Instagram and have at least a couple of 'stories' up every single day. 'And some days that doesn't happen,' she adds, 'but that's just being human.'

'And does it feel like work?' I ask. 'I think it's 100% a form of work,' she says, pushing the soup bowl aside. 'I don't think it's natural to share every ounce of your life. And I especially don't think it's natural to share when you're not doing well, which is actually where I've had success – with being very vulnerable.'

Maintaining an authentic 'personal brand', sometimes across multiple platforms at once, is particularly exhausting. As the anthropologist Ilana Gershon points out, authenticity becomes important when people start to think of themselves as a business. People only tend to worry about portraying an authentic self, she writes, 'when they are faced with the dilemma of marketing themselves as if they were Diet Coke.' One of the ways in which athletes try to resist becoming defined by the brands they are partnered with is to occasionally post content that doesn't fit with a value system that is dependent upon likes and engagement. As Parker puts it in his interview with me:

> So for instance I took a silly selfie yesterday and just posted about how great my workout went. And I know that's not going to do well, I know that's not going to blow up and it's not what everyone wants to see. But I was happy about my workout and wanted to tell everyone about it, so I just was going to do what I was going to do. So I think that shows that I have balance, that I'm not always curating a message to people. Having a stupid selfie like that takes down your

Instagram and brings it back from being so professional and so, like, unrealistic all the time. It's not going to get likes, it's something intangible, it's not going to get likes, but it creates the sense of this is a real person I'm following and it's not always this perfectly photographed photo he's going to post all the time.

Here the challenge is to wrestle a sense of himself back from the persona created for social media. Whilst many athletes find they have most success posting about moments of vulnerability, other athletes I spoke to are less comfortable using social media as a space for opening up about when they are struggling. For one international trail runner, whilst he feels that it is necessary to be what he referred to as a '360-degree' athlete, sharing as much of his training as possible as well as his daily life with his partner and dog, continuing to post during difficult periods can be a challenge. 'During lockdowns I was injured for bits and pieces,' he says. 'Did I make it look like I was still training 100 miles a week and smashing life? Yes. Was I hating life and probably a bit depressed and anxious about getting back into training? Yes.'

There is a tension, he says, between being 'relatable' and sharing the same kinds of injury niggles that all runners get, and providing the kind of 'aspirational' content many people go to social media in search of. 'Do you want to see a professional athlete who you look up to, who's a role model to you, moping about still in their pyjamas at 10.42 in the morning?' he asks rhetorically. From the many conversations I've had with athletes about which posts are most popular, the answer to that question actually seems to be a resounding 'yes' – the best 'performing' posts on Instagram are those that document the highest highs and the lowest lows, the *extremes* of life as an endurance athlete. In many ways this makes sense – the line between peak performance and injury is extremely fine, and 'comeback' narratives are both extremely common and often compelling. But documenting moments of real vulnerability, or the struggle of returning from injury, can be emotionally as well as physically draining. Many endurance athletes are naturally quite introverted, so this requires its own form of endurance.

For this particular athlete, though, who counts among his sponsors an energy drink company that values the portrayal of relentless energy and enthusiasm, it is important to focus on 'aspirational' content. 'After all,' he says, 'my sponsors aren't paying for me to be in rehab, they're paying me to win races.' In fact, it seems like they are paying him for both, as the most successful narratives are usually those of comeback or redemption. One of the professional running teams in America, for example, posted a series of images on Instagram that documented injury alongside victory – a runner struggling through an aqua jogging session in the pool juxtaposed with the same athlete, arms outstretched, streaking through a finish line.

These were some of the most 'high performing' posts they have ever done in terms of likes and engagement on Instagram. According to one member of the group, the perfect 'formula' for a post is 'where you're willing to be vulnerable whilst having that high-performance success.' This does make quite a lot of sense – it resonates with the experience of illness and injury that every endurance athlete goes through at some point. 'If you just post a photo with "Olympic Champion" people are like, "Oh my gosh, amazing" and they'll maybe post "Congrats" underneath it,' he goes on. 'But if you say, "Olympic champion and earlier this year stress fracture but never gave up" then all of a sudden it's a story, you know.'

But what kind of story is this? It aligns with the kind of slogans favoured by major companies involved in endurance sport, epitomised by the Adidas slogan 'Impossible is nothing' and reinforced by notions of relentlessness and exponential improvement (think of Garmin's 'Beat yesterday'). For the most part, these social media posts reinforce 'neoliberal' ideas – that we are all competing against each other and our success or failure is due entirely to our ability to take responsibility for ourselves and work as hard as possible. Inequalities between people are then seen as deserved, rather than as resulting from any kind of economic, racial or gendered barriers.

You see a lot of messages like, 'My life didn't give me what I wanted, it gave me what I worked for' or Mo Farah's 'Don't dream of winning, train for it.' These establish the narrative that hard work equals success and that anyone can achieve anything if they just work hard enough, which is patently false. These kinds of messages are often combined with quotations like 'Overtrain until it's not overtraining', which push a narrative that suggests there is no such thing as overwork, that it is possible to get used to anything, which is dangerous if applied to both running and other aspects of life.

But let's return to the idea that posting on Instagram is 'work'. For Dana and the other athletes I interviewed it literally *is* work – sponsorship contracts with major brands now contain increasingly detailed stipulations about the frequency of posts on social media, and the expectations for engagement and analytics. The hashtags – things like #UnlockYourBest, #EarnIt, #Endurance and #BeatYesterday – that are put into circulation by brands and sponsored athletes, are picked up and reproduced by a whole range of social media users who are not being paid to do so.

The posts and captions themselves also follow what philosopher and anthropologist Bruno Latour called 'scripts', as amateur runners and cyclists mimic the kind of posts that have worked well for professional athletes. It was the American futurist Alvin Toffler who coined that term 'prosumption' in the 1980s to describe an individual who both produces and consumes at the same time, and our use of Instagram and other social media platforms epitomises this. We think of ourselves as consuming images and entertainment from the platform, and yet we ourselves are the ones who create the content So when we post on Facebook we are, in effect, providing free labour for these companies by producing the content that boosts their advertising revenue.

Looking at some of the thousands of endurance-focused Instagram accounts reveals the circulation of a particular kind of 'script' or certain templates for posts that people tend to follow. The media scholar Alice Marwick notes that this tends to 'privilege the kinds of information sharing that benefit corporations more than individuals,' because people tend to copy 'sponsored' posts. These 'scripts' are in one sense fairly simple ones. As one of my interviewees put it, an elite athlete aiming to satisfy their sponsor's requirements might 'just hire a photographer and change their clothes twice and get 30 photos' in one session before tagging their sponsors in a series of posts featuring them running somewhere beautiful in brand-new clothing over the next couple of weeks.

What is interesting about the way these 'scripts' circulate on Instagram is the idea that someone (and not just the corporation with their logo on the apparel) might be trying to sell you something is now very much a part of that script, and therefore ideas about being an authentic athlete are tied up in being an effective and convincing salesperson. It is also significant that the posts of amateur runners who are in no way remunerated for wearing the clothing of a particular brand mimic these posts and hashtags, in a sense paying for the products and then providing free advertising for the companies.

These images can often be beautiful and inspiring, and social media can also forge connections with people and allow us to learn from each other. The problem with social media as a site to learn about endurance sports (and for many beginners it is a key one) is that it tends to amplify particular ideas in ways that can be quite unhelpful.

For instance, at the time of writing my X feed is full of discussions about 'zone 2' training – that is, training at a low intensity according to your heart rate. There are problems with relying on heart rate to determine your training anyway, as I showed in chapter 3, but I have also been on X long enough to remember when my feed was mostly concerned with 'high intensity interval training'. With running we have also seen a shift from minimalist footwear like the *huaraches* worn by Mexico's Rarámuri runners to the maximalist footwear exemplified by the Nike Alphafly, which elevate people high off the ground. It makes sense that the pendulum swings between extremes like this, but it is also useful to remind ourselves that it is happening and being sold to us, and to remember that there is some middle ground.

Particularly extreme opinions are elevated on X because people are more likely to engage – positively or negatively – with them. I think of this as a kind of 'Piers Morgan effect' where the opinion expressed is probably not even necessarily what the author believes, but is something that they know will provoke a reaction. A good example of this is the following from an American coach: 'Runners – if you drink alcohol more than x2 per month, you are basically telling your body/coach/teammates that you don't care about becoming a better runner.' By ignoring all the other ways runners show their commitment to their sport and teammates, this seems designed almost entirely to provoke. By this logic a whole host of past stars of the sport, from Steve Prefontaine to Rod Dixon ('All I want to do is drink beer and train like an animal'), would be off the team.

Another example comes from a physiologist who, according to his bio, uses data, science and AI to facilitate maximum athletic development: 'Some coaches chase fatigue. I avoid it like the plague. By the time an athlete can perceive fatigue, their ability to respond to the training is already compromised.' This is clearly well intentioned and has the aim of protecting the athlete, but it also seems designed to generate a response. As Charlie Spedding noted, training seriously means coping with a level of fatigue all the time – and he won an Olympic medal in the marathon. Certainly in my own experience there is no way of running 100 miles in a week without feeling tired most of the time. The problem with this kind of polarisation is that we lose nuance in the process, but also that extreme views are amplified, which can make things seem more complicated than they need to be.

It goes without saying that a lot of social media activity, particularly from sponsored athletes, is really about selling us things. For running especially, as a sport that – at least until the recent introduction of expensive wearable technology and super shoes – can still be extremely cheap, this usually involves selling us things we don't really need. Many of the posts of professional athletes now feature references to the kinds of technologies I wrote about at length earlier in this book, because these companies often have venture capital money to spend on convincing amateur athlete consumers that they are necessary for their success.

One athlete, who was sponsored by a leading wearable technology company, explained that there was more engagement with posts that just gave a tantalising glimpse of data about metrics like 'strain' and 'recovery'. 'That draws more people in,' he explained, 'because people are like, "I want to see more of that" or "I want to have that for myself."' Access to this kind of data is clearly compelling and yet the professional athletes I have spoken to are themselves somewhat sceptical about the constant use of wearable technology and the effects of sharing too much information, even as their sponsors encourage them to make more and more intimate data available.

Their scepticism is twofold. Firstly, athletes are concerned about the effects on their own performance that could arise as a result of an over-reliance on wearable technology. In the days leading up to a big race, when it is quite normal to get a little less sleep and feel a little more on edge, they spoke to me about removing devices that measure HRV. 'The last thing you want is your watch telling you that you're not ready to perform on the morning of a race,' as one runner puts it.

Perhaps more importantly, many athletes are concerned about normalising the sharing of data that could actually be quite intimate. As one athlete, whose team were being encouraged to share the data from wearable technology openly on social media, says, 'There's definitely some guys on our team who struggle with their sleep and they struggle with various things like anxiety throughout the day, and sharing that kind of data and the reasons it might spike or plummet for a certain reason might be a bit close to home.'

Others note that access to raw data also potentially allows people to detect a whole range of things, from whether an athlete has consumed alcohol to whether or not they are menstruating. What seems to be happening is that the companies sponsoring elite endurance athletes are encouraging not only the production of this kind of data, but also its widespread dissemination. When athletes who are sponsored by wearable technology companies are encouraged to post their heart rate data and information about their sleep patterns, they are altering the 'script' of endurance-based social media posting in particular ways and normalising this kind of sharing.

What might the effects of this information about the day-to-day lives of elite athletes be? In cycling there is speculation that widely available training data, shared on apps like Strava, is partly responsible for a new wave of ultra-talented youngsters making it to the front of the peloton quicker than previous generations, because they knew at an earlier age exactly what was required to succeed: how many watts, for how long, up exactly what percentage gradient. In this sense, the information is liberating, clearing the path to the top for those with enough ability.

For others, though, seeing how fast professional runners train could be extremely off-putting. As the American athlete Sam Parsons sees it, 'Having that readily available data pushes everything forward in terms of performance, but I do think it's a double-edged sword. Too much data, too much information, might actually take people's love out of the sport earlier. I didn't have social media from an early age with running and I don't know if I was seeing "Holy crap, these people are running a five-minute-per-mile pace on their tempo runs and I'm only doing six-minute miles" that might have deterred me from continuing with the sport.'

Both young athletes observing these posts on sites such as Instagram *and* the athletes themselves often experience sharing this kind of data as anxiety producing. This all means that the peripheral 'work' of being an endurance athlete (that is, the work that is not actually training and racing) ends up feeling like an endurance challenge in its own right; one that is experienced as a distraction from and detriment to the actual work of running or cycling. For us amateur endurance athletes, it is worth remembering that whilst professional athletes might increasingly have to treat themselves as brands, we don't have to.

8

ON RUNNING AND BEING HUMAN

One of the explanations I have heard most frequently for the boom in ultra-distance running is the idea that we were 'born' to run; that there is not only something innately human in setting one foot in front of the other, but that this act in some sense makes us who we are. The connection between endurance and evolution was often invoked as a justification for spending so much time training. I have often wondered, though, whether in our desire to substantiate the deep connection we feel with running, we sometimes try to construct a version of both 'nature' and human history that matches our intuitions rather than reality.

Many of these ideas about the connection between running and evolution, or running and being human, have a relatively short history. Many can be traced to a paper in *Nature* that was published in 2006 by two Americans, the biologist Dennis Bramble and the paleoanthropologist Dan Lieberman, who in turn sought to answer questions posed by a previous generation of biologists, such as Russell Newman, author of the wonderfully titled paper, 'Why is man such a sweaty and thirsty naked animal?'

In their paper, 'Endurance running and the evolution of homo', Bramble and Lieberman argue that the reason we're so sweaty and naked is that other aspects of our biology and anatomy have combined to enable us to outrun other animals over long distances, and therefore made us better hunters. They do so through looking at our anatomy now alongside a careful examination of the fossil record, aiming to pinpoint when particular adaptations to do with energetics (how efficiently we can move), strength (how resilient we are to high impacts), stabilisation (for example, how well we can support our head whilst running and how our arms help us balance) and thermoregulation (how we keep ourselves cool) developed.

For example, they note that the particular formation of the nuchal ligament in the neck, which helps us hold our head steady as we run, was first identifiable in a 1.9 million-year-old *homo habilis* skull called 'KNM-ER 1813', discovered in Kenya in 1973. They take these specific adaptations, which seem to imply that we became progressively more suited to long-distance running, and speculate that they gave us an advantage in 'exploit[ing] protein-rich resources such as meat, marrow and brain' by either allowing us to run animals to exhaustion, get close enough to throw projectiles at them or run to scavenging opportunities more quickly.

Both authors of the paper were keen runners and it is easy to see why this idea is so appealing. I have certainly had moments of 'flow' when it feels like running long distances is precisely what my body was for, and it has always felt like waking up and running at dawn is the best way to start a day. In the *Nature* paper Bramble and Lieberman do mention some doubts – for instance that hunting using endurance running is too 'energetically expensive and low-yield for the benefits to have outweighed the costs.'

I have always been curious about this theory for several reasons. Firstly, I wonder how likely it is that we actually relied on persistence hunting (tracking an animal by running over long periods of time until the animal becomes exhausted) given what we know about modern hunter-gatherers and the kind of environments it's likely we evolved in. Second, how does the idea that we evolved to run change the way we think about and characterise modern hunter-gatherers like the Hadza in Tanzania, and other populations associated with running like the Rarámuri? And, perhaps most importantly, given that the main considerations for evolutionary anthropologists tend to be how much energy is expended for the amount of food that is acquired, what other reasons might there have been for running? What other kinds of meaning might people have derived from it?

The 'endurance hypothesis' I've outlined here has become particularly popular due to the compelling storytelling of Chris McDougall's *Born to Run*. McDougall is the latest and best-known writer to attempt to explain Rarámuri running primarily in terms of our evolutionary past, and to ask how they compare to other runners around the world. In fact, the race he describes in 2006, in which my new Rarámuri friends Silvino and Arnulfo competed against America's best ultra-marathon runners, was only the latest in a long series of encounters organised by Americans.

On 7 November 1925 two Rarámuri runners, Zafiro and San Miguel, ran 100km from Pachuca to Mexico City in nine hours and 26 minutes, in a feat that was described breathlessly in the *New York Times* as having 'no parallel in sporting history'. They ran with the Mexican flag embroidered on their vests along new asphalt highways. 'Long life to you, gladiators of the Mexican woodlands!' shouted onlookers as they passed through Tulpedac on a run that was strikingly political. Not long after Mexico's long and bloody revolution, Zafiro and San Miguel's journey symbolised a new commitment to *indigenismo*, the incorporation of indigenous people into the mainstream of Mexican life.

Many people were keen to capitalise on the two runners' abilities. Promoters organised a bleak-sounding contest in Kansas that pitted them against the Navajo and the Apache to determine the 'world's hardiest aboriginal'. Vaudeville agents took them on a national tour, exhibiting them in front of dramatic backdrops resembling the Sierra Madre. Then several months later they set off again to run even further, 82 miles, from San Antonio to Austin, Texas, in a run sponsored by Pontiac cars ('famous for long life and economy in endurance tests'). The Mexican government even pushed for the introduction of a 100km event in the Olympics and we can only wonder how different ultra-distance running would look today had it been successful.

These runs took place at the same time as dance marathons were capturing the attention of the American public and the fascination was just as acute. In the final stages of their 82-mile run, Zafiro and San Miguel were slowed to a walk by the sheer number of people and cars that had amassed to accompany them, whilst horse-mounted police struggled to keep the route open. As Mark Dyreson puts it in his *Journal of Sports History* article on the subject, 'In a decade in which machines were obliterating traditional notions of time and distance, the fascination with the Rarámuri involved modern anxieties and expectations.' Amongst these: 'Would the automobile and the airplane render the human body obsolete? Would technology make human abilities insignificant?'

These are questions which, with the advent of AI and the increasing embrace of wearable technology and performance medicine, are even more pertinent today. Today people aren't trying to use the Rarámuri to sell Pontiac cars, they are using them to sell minimalist running sandals and chia seeds, but in many ways very little has changed in a hundred years. Zafiro and San

Miguel ran respectably for Mexico in the 1928 Olympic marathon in Amsterdam, although it wasn't made clear to them that the race was a mere 26 miles long. They continued to run after the finish line, only to eventually be halted by volunteers.

Their lament that the race was 'too short, too short' is very similar to Silvino's feelings about the race depicted in *Born to Run*, but recorded almost a century earlier. It is perhaps no surprise that the Rarámuri retreated out of the spotlight again until feature stories in publications like *National Geographic* rekindled interest in the 1960s. These brought with them a renewed interest in the supposed 'natural' physiological abilities of the Rarámuri, yet whilst studies demonstrated that regular *rarájipari* players showed extremely high aerobic capacity, that of the Rarámuri who attended local mission schools was the same as their classmates, indicating that this was likely to be a result of lifestyle rather than genetics.

Newspapers in the 1920s tended to ascribe the endurance capabilities of Rarámuri runners to a freedom from the 'blandishments of civilisation' as one put it, painting them as 'noble savages' in Rousseau's terms, representatives of an imagined Garden of Eden. More recent depictions combine this kind of characterisation with the assumption that they represent a stage of our evolutionary past.

This attempt to rank groups of people according to their place on an evolutionary ladder using sports is one that anthropology as a discipline is historically inescapably bound up in. The 1904 Olympic Games was held as part of the World's Fair in St Louis, Missouri, and the exhibitions at the fair included 'living villages' where people from various societies lived in enclosures and practised preindustrial indigenous customs for the entertainment of thousands of visitors. A 'Special Olympics' was organised alongside the Olympic Games by anthropologists explicitly to make comparisons between these so-called 'primitive' people and Caucasian athletes who had been trained in Western-style competitions.

The purpose of this, as President of the American Anthropological Association at the time WJ McGee put it, was to display the 'many long chapters of human evolution', whilst positioning white Americans at the peak of the evolutionary pyramid. It didn't matter to the organisers that the competitors from the 'living villages' were often reluctant to participate, or that they were competing against the best American athletes who had trained for many years – the Games fulfilled their purpose.

Today the tendency is usually to do the opposite, to claim that the representatives of the 'Stone Age' as McDougall puts it, are *better* runners than we are, but this serves the same purpose of defining ourselves in opposition to who we are not and positions groups of people on a scale of advancement. These ways of thinking about our evolutionary past also tend to lump together a range of different hunter-gatherers from different parts of the world, and to collapse ancient and modern hunter-gatherers together, depriving modern hunter-gatherers of their modernity. In making his argument that we are 'born to run' McDougall also applies Bramble and Lieberman's work in palaeoanthropology, intended to analyse hunter-gatherer lifestyles, to the Rarámuri, who have been practising agriculture for thousands of years.

As Noa Lavi, Alice Rudge and Graeme Warren argue in a recent paper in *Current Anthropology*, the mismatch between modern lifestyles and those of idealised hunter-gatherers are normally recruited in order to sell us things, from diets to training courses in survival skills. Hunter-gatherers thus represent 'both our evolutionary past and an ideal future state in which "we" become "natural" and "wild" – just like "they" are supposed to be.' They also note that it tends to be the marketable aspects of hunter-gatherer lifestyles that are emphasised, rather than those that go against the capitalist status quo. It is rare, for example, that you hear calls for us to return to our ancestral pasts by bringing back 'demand sharing', where a community shares pooled resources according to need without an expectation of repayment.

I remain intrigued by the evolutionary hypotheses outlined in *Born to Run*, though, not least because so many of the people I have spoken to about ultra-running talk about feeling that we were designed in some way to do this. So, did we evolve to run long distances? This is an ongoing discussion amongst evolutionary anthropologists. For some it has similarities to the widely discredited 'aquatic ape' hypothesis, the theory that our ancestors once spent significant amounts of time in the water, evidenced by our lack of hair, a subcutaneous fat layer and other characteristics. Critics of the running theory point out that it begins with physiological characteristics then works backwards, trying to find evidence of humans running long distances in old accounts by anthropologists, of which there are actually very few.

Amongst contemporary hunter-gatherer societies, there are only four or five that have been documented to hunt in this way and none that still do so regularly. Supporters of the endurance running theory would say that this is a modern bias, as the ethnographic record (detailed accounts of the ways in which people in particular cultures live) only stretches back a century or so to a time when people already had access to more 'modern' methods of hunting (the use of ranged weapons for hunting is actually extremely ancient, going back at least 60,000 years). It could also be the case that persistence hunting has been curtailed by modern practices that enclose land.

As Duncan Stibbard-Hawkes, a colleague of mine in evolutionary anthropology at Durham University who works mainly with the Hadza in Tanzania, puts it, persistence hunting gets harder if you don't have wide-open spaces, because 'otherwise you're chasing a kangaroo into a thicket and that's no good.' Here he defines 'wide-open' space as areas where there are no trees, bushes or other places for animals to hide, and he questions whether there was actually significantly more space like this in the past than there is now. Reconstructions of the African environments in which we evolved suggest they were savanna woodlands, often covered by grasses, which would have made tracking difficult, rather than the wide open, baking-hot spaces in which persistence hunting works best.

* * *

The Hadza are one of the tribes associated with persistence running today, to the extent that a race has even been organised in Tanzania (by a company somewhat predictably called Barefoot Adventures) to allow ultra-runners to experience something of Hadza life first-hand. 'The racers will forage for wild berries,' reads a BBC article on the subject, 'dig for tubers, hand-make arrows, harvest honey and climb the baobab trees for water and fruit.'

Through Duncan's contacts with the Hadza I am able to speak to Endeko, a member of the Hadza tribe who works as a research assistant and translator, who has first-hand experience of the transformation of Hadza land and hunting practices. He hasn't heard of the race. 'When I think of racing I think of people competing for money and driving in cars,' he says. 'We don't really race here.' Contrary to what might be expected, though, he says there is often more running involved in hunting now than in the recent past. 'There are fewer animals since the Hadza land has been invaded by pastoralists and agriculturalists,' is how he puts it. 'Climate change has also caused many problems and now we have to chase the animals in order to kill them because of the lower number of animals in the bush.'

I ask whether it's important to be considered a strong runner in Hadza culture. 'Of course it is important,' he says. 'People who can run after animals and kill them are considered heroes.' He emphasises the fact that there is no out-and-out persistence hunting anymore, though, and that there may never have been. People are more likely to weaken animals with poisoned arrows before they run them down, and the use of poison, like more sophisticated hunting techniques, is ancient. Stories about running prowess are important, he says, and often told with great gusto. Again, though, they are not quite what we might expect. The stories the Hadza tell are 'more likely to be about being chased than about chasing,' he explains.

The Hadza live in close proximity with elephants and buffalo, both of which can be extremely dangerous. 'If you sit down with the elders,' Endeko says, 'they'll tell you all about how they escaped from elephants. For example Maloba was hunting and he crossed paths with a group of elephants. They saw him and started to chase him. He's short, and when he ran his knees knocked his mouth and broke his teeth, but he still didn't stop. He climbed a hill and stopped to breathe there. He still doesn't have his two front teeth.'

Stories of running away – whether it be from rain showers, bees or elephants – are perhaps a little less inspiring than those about persistence hunting in explaining what it means to be human. I'm also not sure we can make assumptions about the past based on the behaviour of contemporary hunter-gatherers. If we can, though, it seems more likely that persistence hunting was one technique among many, probably only used by some groups where the environment was appropriate for it.

The lament that our lives today are too sedentary, and that this goes against the way that humans have lived for thousands of years, does seem fair, and the Hadza are certainly far more active than the majority of people with desk jobs, they're just not endurance hunters. The idea so often depicted on t-shirts, with an ape gradually standing upright, launching into a run and then hunching reluctantly over a desk, is overly simplistic. However, this notion of evolution as goal-oriented and always associated with progress is both wrong and outdated.

'A proper evolutionary anthropologist will tell you that evolution doesn't aim towards a particular end point,' is how Duncan puts it. 'It doesn't march forward on a pre-ordained path, right? It fits to environments.' We can say with some certainty that humans evolved in complex social and environmental niches in which we had to use a huge amount of intelligence to feed ourselves. Interestingly, some recent research has shown that under 'periods of energetic stress' – in this case 250km ultramarathons in Jordan and Sri Lanka – the performance of athletes' brains actually improved in tasks relating to foraging, such as storing location information and navigation. This is quite a remarkable example of 'cognitive plasticity' developed over the course of just a few days, although Duncan is sceptical about the longer-term effects: over extended periods of time malnutrition definitely doesn't make us smarter.

So maybe navigation and tracking skills were more important adaptations than pure endurance. In *The Art of Tracking*, the evolutionary biologist Louis Liebenberg argues that, fundamentally, modern scientists and trackers require the same reasoning processes and intellectual abilities, but nonetheless tracking involves a high level of skill, and an intimate knowledge of animal behaviour and the surrounding environment, built up over the course of a lifetime. Liebenberg notes that a group of !Xo trackers, hunter-gatherers who live primarily in the Kalahari region of Botswana and Namibia, were able to identify the footprints of individual animals and people, finding it 'very amusing that [he] should ask them such a stupid question.'

They would use persistence hunting techniques to hunt various animals depending on the time of year and condition of the ground, but crucially, Liebeberg writes, 'the success of this method relies on how quickly the animal can be tracked down.' As Duncan suggests, this largely depends on the ground: if it has been heavily stripped of cover by cattle grazing, the prey is easier to follow, but if the ground is too wooded it becomes difficult to track quickly enough. If the animals are able to escape into woodland the risk of failure becomes too great. In the cases Liebenberg writes about it is always tracking ability, rather than pure endurance, that determines success or failure.

And it's not just about the hunting itself. In much of the Kalahari, according to Liebenberg, hunting in this way involved a great expenditure of energy for few returns, but it nevertheless 'holds a central place in the community and camp life.' Knowledge and experience are shared in lengthy and gripping descriptions around the campfire, and 'artistic expression is involved in relating events in an entertaining way.' For many groups, being a good hunter also requires demonstrating humility and gentleness. For instance, amongst the Ju/Wasi, who live in a similar region to the !Xo described above, announcing a kill is seen as a show of arrogance and successful hunters deliberately alternate periods of hunting with periods of inactivity (to 'cool their hearts and make them gentle'), which allow others in the group to reciprocate. Hunting, then, in these examples, doesn't seem to follow a competitive, survival-of-the-fittest logic at all.

The symbolic and mythological aspects of tracking and hunting animals are also extremely important. Part of the imaginative process of tracking often involves hunters identifying themselves with the animal, speculating on what they would have done had they been in their place. The anthropologist Mathias Guenther has noted the similarities between the running hunter and the shaman entering into a trance state. Both involve 'extreme physical exertion, intensely felt.' He quotes a !Xo hunter named Karoha, who makes the point succinctly, and echoes the sentiment of many Rarámuri runners I spoke to: 'Tracking is like dancing, because your body is happy.'

As the hunt reaches its conclusion, both hunter and hunted begin to reach the limits of their endurance, and it is at this point that their identities begin to merge. 'What you will see,' Karoha explains, speaking about hunting kudu, 'is that you are now controlling its mind. You are getting its mind. The eyes are no longer wild. You have taken the kudu into your mind.' At this point, in fact, both hunter and hunted are understood to be close to death. When the hunter returns to camp, they are revived with water in a kind of symbolic rebirth.

In terms of how easy it is to acquire meat, then, this kind of hunting does not seem very practical, although it clearly has a role to play in reinforcing the connection between humans and animals, and is an important part of the way the !Xo and other peoples see the world. However, we shouldn't necessarily think of these practices purely in terms of evolutionary adaptability. As Duncan says, 'Whilst we're good at optimising, there's not some kind of omniscient evolutionary gremlin on your shoulder saying "Do this, it's adaptive."' As the examples in this chapter show, rather than telling a simple story about evolution, beliefs about running are diverse, and it may be that the social and ritual values of this kind of running are more important than its value as a hunting strategy, or even that people do it primarily because it is enjoyable.

So hunting in this way may have been passed on from generation to generation, kept alive through practice and camp-fire stories in a process of what anthropologists call 'cultural evolution'. The egalitarian practice of successful hunters deliberately taking a back seat to allow others to reciprocate, as well as the broader social and symbolic value of hunting in this way, make the kinds of questions many people ask about persistence hunting and various other 'traditional' running practices seem misplaced. Time and time again, the question about the Rarámuri and others has been the same. For example, an article about a foot race that accompanied a dance ceremony was published in 1902 in the *San Francisco Chronicle* with the title 'Are Mocqui runners world beaters?' From reading accounts of running in these places, it doesn't seem to be a question that would interest many of those actually engaged in races, ceremonies or persistence hunts, and what stands out is that the reasons for running are actually quite varied and only loosely connected to practices like endurance hunting, but tracing the ways that people have made running meaningful seems like an important thing to do, and hopefully sheds some light on the (possibly narrower) range of meanings running has for us today.

According to Peter Nabokov, author of *Indian Running*, about the traditions of Native Americans, including the Hopi tribe of

Arizona, 'Running and fertility are so entwined in Hopi consciousness that the one action generally implies the other.' Running forms an element of almost all group prayers for rain and growth, often particularly onerous and potentially dangerous running. One ritual, for instance, calls for a brave man to impersonate the original owner of Hopi lands, the deity of fire. To do so, the man who is chosen must spend four days in seclusion, eating only corn in order to 'become skinny and a fast runner,' emerging each night at midnight to run in successively tightening circles, 'corralling the clouds almost as if they were wild horses,' Nabokov describes.

Hopi farms – like those of the Rarámuri – were often long distances from their villages, requiring them to carry tools, food and water up and down several mesas. Running was an efficient way of travelling between village and crops, especially on the sandy surface that often covered the trails. But it was more than just a mode of transport. Hopi chiefs believed that healthy crops required runners to run with happy hearts and to run swiftly, so that the rain clouds would follow them to their fields. Running ability was therefore not just a by-product of an existence that required a high expenditure of energy. Instead, it emerged from strong beliefs about the interactions between people and their environment.

In many cultures the act of running has a far greater significance than merely transforming the individual who performed it. The Rarámuri tell a story about God, at the very beginning of time, organising the first race, between a deer and a frog. The deer tried to cheat by putting the frog in a box, but the frog escaped and won. In the beginning the earth was muddy and soft, and races like this hardened the earth and made it habitable, in the same way that the feet of runners and dancers do today.

Among the Navajo of the southwestern United States to run was to join with the motion that is at the heart of life itself. Ceremonial running makes the connection between running, the ceaselessness of motion and the lifeforce. In pueblos such as Taos and Picuris in New Mexico the traditional running race tracks follow 'sun roads' aligned with the movement of the sun across the sky. Two teams would start in the east, racing for the west end of the track to tag the next runner in the relay. This would continue back and forth until one team gained an entire lap. These races were fiercely competitive, but the competition was designed to strengthen community bonds as the runners worked together for cosmic regeneration. Like Rarámuri *rarájipari* races, the aim was for them to continue for a long time.

DH Lawrence went along to watch some of these races in the 1920s and wrote that the runners do not race for a prize or for themselves. He wrote of the running he witnessed combining anguish and ecstasy, and focused on the purpose of this effort, which was to fuel a creative energy that would sustain the tribe in the months ahead. This is a somewhat romantic account, but it does capture something important: that the social value of running in this context is more important than anything else. People ran not for themselves, but for the continued prosperity of their tribe.

I have spoken to many people about what makes running meaningful to them and they nearly all talk with a hint of embarrassment about the 'cliché' of wanting to feel a connection with nature, but it's clear that this has often been an explicit aim of running. The anthropologist Thomas Buckley explains that the Yurok people, Native Americans who traditionally lived in what is now California, attempted to create an 'extrasensory' relationship with the trails they ran on, speaking and even singing to them.

They were taught to think of the trail as an active being, allowing it to dictate the run 'as though the trail was running out behind them and under them by itself.' This could be practised by running along the trail with your eyes closed, trusting it to guide you.

This was also achieved through visualisation, as the runner was taught to feel the ground pushing up under their feet rather than their feet pushing down on the ground. If they could imagine that it was the world's energies that were being used rather than their own, they could get to a point where 'the running is just happening; whether the world is doing it or you are doing it is of no importance.' It is easy to see how this way of thinking about the self could help people to run extraordinary distances: if you're running on the energy of the whole world rather than just your own body it must feel like you could run forever.

Running has also long been a way of carrying other kinds of messages over long distances. Many other Native American tribes, including the Sauk, Kickapoo and Mesquakie, had courier corps of ceremonial runners who would deliver messages. Often from high-ranking families, they alone had the right to deliver the deciding vote on deadlocked councils. In South America, the Inca had a complex system of trails and post stations called the *chasqui*, with runners delivering news at lightning speed in two-mile sections. During the civil wars that followed the Spanish conquest, messages could travel 150 miles a day in this fashion. Whilst the Spanish mail (carried on horseback) took 12 days to reach Lima from Cusco, the runners could do it in three.

More recently, the Hopi have been forced to advocate for other things, for example by sending a team of runners the 265 miles to Phoenix to protest against the coal company Peabody's use of water from an aquifer that was causing their wells to dry up. When the

World Water Forum was held in Mexico City a delegation ran there, covering 1800 miles in total. The anthropologist Peter Nabokov tells the story of a young boy who became the last ceremonial runner of the Mesquakie tribe. On the 13th day of a fast he was visited by a hummingbird. 'I give you the quality of willingness,' the hummingbird said. 'I also give you the quality of tranquil braveness.' The holy gift of speed came at a price, however: 'You must live morally in the future.'

It is not enough, then, just to carry messages. This is a role that involves living in a certain way and embodying particular values, something like a running monk. When a Hopi runner sets off to run for rain, they are enacting a desire for what they want to happen. They not only carry their message, but they become the message. 'To some degree,' Nabokov writes, 'he turns into rain-cloud-blown-by-wind.' He doesn't run like the wind, he is the wind. One of the main reasons given by the Rarámuri for the decline in *rarájipari* races is that they no longer had the desired effect of making it rain, the climate having become so unpredictable. Today, though, an increasingly large group of endurance athletes have their own message about the climate to transmit, and they are finding that to carry it, whilst doing extremely difficult things, can be an effective way to raise awareness about the climate crisis. I come back to this theme at the end of the book. Now, though, we go somewhere with a far more recent trail running culture: Nepal.

9

SINDHUPALCHOK, NEPAL

'Eat well, move well, enjoy'

— *Mira Rai, Nepali trail runner*

I sit on the wall outside an imposing metal gate that I thought was the entrance to Gokarna Sahid Smarak Park, but which, given that Will and Lopsang are not here, is probably not the right entrance to Gokarna Sahid Smarak Park. This is one of a number of times on this trip that I regret not getting a local sim card – sometimes meeting up the old-fashioned way just doesn't work out. A very expensive couple of minutes of data roaming later, Will and I work out the problem: I'm at the park's upper entrance, and he and Lopsang are at the lower one, a few hundred metres below me. Will sighs. 'We'll jog up and find you,' he says.

The path I came up in the taxi is pretty steep, so I'm quite pleased to be sitting on the wall with a little glass of black coffee rather than running up it, and grateful for any slight advantage I can gain to compensate for the jet lag and lack of acclimatisation to the altitude. Ten minutes or so later they arrive, Will in wraparound shades and a running vest looking very different to how he's looked in our previous encounters in academic seminars. Lopsang wears a bright red vest and a pair of Asics road running shoes, evidence that trail running shoes are as hard to come by here in Nepal as they are in Ethiopia.

We walk for a couple of minutes before Lopsang breaks into a run up a narrow trail, which starts almost immediately to rise so steeply that it is cut with small steps. It is not long before I am breathing pretty hard – I've only been at altitude for a couple of days, but until now I hadn't noticed it as much in Kathmandu as I used to when I arrived in Addis. Lopsang notices and, turning, he says, 'Welcome to Nepali trail,' before returning his attention to the task at hand. I am struck by the fact that this is almost exactly what Silvino had said to me when the trail started to get difficult in Mexico. These hills and the idiosyncrasies of the trails that have been forged across them are assets and might even be particularly precious ones in the quest to compete on trail running's emerging global stage.

We follow a ridge up into the forest, which is draped with so many multi-coloured prayer flags that at some points we have to duck to avoid them. They flutter above us and the effect is of running through a green and garlanded tunnel, the sky briefly visible in gaps between the trees. It is hard, though, to look up. The trail is punctuated by large round boulders of chalky white rock. Luckily this turns out to be quite grippy, almost as though the rocks are a particularly well-frequented bouldering spot. But they are big and I keep having to break stride to climb over them in ungainly fashion.

Lopsang springs over them like they are some kind of plyometric obstacle. 'I don't know how he does that,' Will says from behind me. 'My legs are much longer than his and I still have to stop.' Lopsang's running style reminds me a little of how the great Nepalise trail runner Mira Rai runs – arms low and compact, but legs full of power, her running resembling more a series of leaps than a monotonous lope. This looks like a huge waste of energy but in fact on trails like this it keeps the momentum going upwards in a way that my more tentative approach does not.

Will is a fell and trail runner from Northumberland who is doing research for his anthropology PhD on Nepalese trail running and he's invited me along for his morning training run with Lopsang. Whilst we met at 7 a.m. to run, Lopsang has been up since 4 a.m. training for the martial art Muay Thai (also known as Thai boxing), his other passion, but this doesn't show. Gokarna, just outside the Kathmandu ring road, is home to several Gurkha training centres as well as training camps for Muay Thai, and we passed the Nepalese national boxing team doing hill sprints on the way up the hill. Having narrowly missed out on selection for the Gurkhas, Lopsang is spreading his bets by continuing to train for both trail running and Muay Thai.

He tells us that his motivation for being an athlete is very similar to his motivation for joining the Gurkhas. It is a way to make a name for himself in the world and ensure that he is never forgotten. Will translates for me as we run. 'He says his grandfather was in the Gurkhas during the Second World War,' between pauses for breath. 'But he suffered so much and saw so many of his friends dying that he talked Lopsang's dad out of joining.' Lopsang keeps talking as he continues to bound up the slope. 'Now though,' Will continues to translate, 'people are already forgetting his father's name, but his grandfather's name is revered within the family and the village because of his heroism during the war.'

Above our heads Nepalese flags flap in the breeze alongside the prayer flags. 'The name of an athlete is the greatest of all,' Will continues. 'So even if he didn't become a Gurkha he can increase his status as an athlete and people will remember him.' Trail running is also a way to leave Nepal and represent Nepal to the world, which is a big motivation for a lot of the runners here, albeit a dream that can be hard to realise.

When there is a break in the trees we can see the outskirts of Kathmandu in the valley below through wispy white cloud. 'What a beautiful trail,' I say to Will. 'It is,' he replies, telling me that he ran for five hours up here a couple of days ago. 'I didn't mean to,' he says, before adding somewhat wistfully, 'but sometimes once I get going I can't stop heading up.' I hope he can today, because I'm going to try to run 60km at the Sindhupalchok International Trail Race in four days' time and my legs are already protesting on this terrain.

It is coming to the end of rainy season in Nepal and in places the trail has been reinforced with now-bursting sandbags. When we hit a patch of road we see evidence of a recent landslide, but luckily most of the trail has now dried out. After the shock of the initial hill the rest of the run is relatively relaxed and I am able to enjoy the views when the demands of the trail allow it. Soon, though, we hit a patch of trail where the earth is red and, just as Lopsang warns me of how slippery it is, the ground skids out from under my feet, and Will nearly hits the deck behind me as well. 'This colour means it's slippery,' Lopsang says helpfully and I'm glad I've got a few days to try to learn to read the ground here. I'm reminded of the subtle details I notice immediately in the UK – the particular white flower that grows on the most treacherous Highland bogs, for instance, and which you know to avoid if you've ever ended up waist deep.

Most of the trail runners here are Rai, Tamang or Gurung, groups of people who come from the 'middle hills', between about

1500m and 2500m above sea level, but I also meet Sherpa runners from the Solu Khumbu higher up the mountains, as well as some runners from the lowlands. For the most part people here have a first name followed by the name of their caste or ethnic group, making it relatively easy to know roughly where they are from – hearing the names Lopsang Tamang, for example, or Mira Rai people would know that they were from the hills.

Will's research centres around the Mira Rai Initiative, an NGO established by the legendary trail runner to provide a structured training environment for a group of young women, as well as lessons in things like English, computing and women's rights. One of the aims of the programme is to bring young women from a range of different parts of Nepal and a range of castes together, allowing them to learn from each other and then, through the 'exchange and empower' programme, to go further afield to share their stories with others, both in Nepal and internationally.

There is definitely a sense in which being from the lowlands is seen by people here as presenting an additional challenge for an up-and-coming trail runner. Catching up to those who are used to the mountain terrain is perceived as a struggle and as I watch Lopsang skip away down the trail I can see why. Much of his Gurkha training – like that of the mountaineer Nirmal Purja – consisted of carrying heavy loads in a basket whilst covering terrain like this at pace for hours on end, so running encumbered by only the lightest of trail running backpacks must feel comparatively easy.

We continue to climb for another 20 minutes or so and the incline gradually and thankfully eases until we are on a plateau and can look down on Kathmandu. The view actually reminds me a lot of Addis Ababa viewed from Mount Entoto: sprawling buildings with a faint cloud cover burning off in the sun and a faint haze from the cars and motorbikes struggling past each other in the streets. The bowl in which Kathmandu sits is wonderfully green, though, and the annual race around its rim must be a lot of fun.

From the top we drop down to an asphalt road which descends the hill in switchbacks and I experience the familiar feeling of being back on home territory, my stride returning to a loping metronome. This doesn't last long, though – why would we take the road down when there are roughly hewn paths cutting vertically down the hill between the switchbacks? We descend via the road for a few minutes at a time followed by a plunge down one of these desire lines, until we eventually emerge back in Gokarna, where Will and Lopsang live, and where the Mira Rai Initiative is based.

After some fresh juice at a roadside juice bar and some very spicy noodles, Will and I head to the Mira Rai Initiative to meet Mira and her current set of protégés. The buildings are clustered closely together in Gokarna, and connected by narrow cobbled streets and winding dirt lanes, and in spite of the fact Will has been here several times before, we are soon lost and have to ask for directions. Eventually we find a tall new building with a couple of mountain bikes and an array of muddy trainers neatly stacked in a shoe rack outside – this must be the place. There are a few pairs of Salomon trail running shoes in the shoe rack, but most are local brands like Magic, a reminder that Mira is the only athlete here who is sponsored.

Anita Rai pads to the door barefoot and lets us in. She is just back from finishing third in the 100km race at the Ultra Tour Monte Rosa in Switzerland. An alumnus of the Initiative, she now helps out on the frequent occasions Mira is away running, lobbying the government for more support or promoting the sport elsewhere.

Obtaining the funds and permissions to run a race abroad is particularly challenging for Nepali athletes and few are able to compete internationally. Mira, in pink shorts and an orange tank top, is positivity personified, in spite of being injured at the moment, and fizzes with energy even more than usual as a result of not being able to run.

'I've been to the UK,' she tells us, before adding 'little, little hills' and laughing. She won the women's race at the Ben Nevis Ultra, finishing in sixth place overall. The young women living here at the moment are part of the fifth cohort of athletes and will graduate after the race in Sindhupalchok at the weekend. We sit in the classroom, which has walls covered in posters the runners have made on themes like gender-based violence and same-sex marriage, as well as lists of 'trail running benefits' (top of the list: 'reconnect with nature'). Will and I ask them about their preparations for the race, and they give an account illustrated with TikTok videos and motivational songs.

Some of these videos feature running, but they also depict other preparations for the race. In one, Padam carefully stacks flat stones into a cairn on the mountainside, before the video cuts to her meditating cross-legged as a torrential downpour falls through the forest canopy above her. In others they draw attention to the music that plays in the background to the videos and which they sometimes sing whilst they are training. These are a combination of Gurkha songs like '*Jaadai Chu Paltanma*,' which translates to something like 'I'm going away to join the army', and the Nepali Maoist music Mira became used to during her time in the army. They describe this as 'making energy'-type music.

Tacked on the notice board is a training plan that consists of a combination of fartlek ('speed play') runs and 'endurance' runs on particularly hilly routes, as well as yoga and leg-strengthening sessions. Mira also encourages the young women to practise martial arts and rock climbing, and some of the other TikTok videos they show us are of them laughing and messing around at a climbing wall in Kathmandu. On the training-plan printout someone has written a slogan in red pen: 'Don't just dream of winning, train for it' it says, a phrase taken from a Nike advertising campaign and attributed to Mo Farah.

This seems a somewhat incongruous choice in an environment that is explicitly oriented towards using running to foster connections with people. The advertising campaigns associated with the slogan are curious in that they feature Farah training completely alone, with voiceovers that emphasise the solitary nature of endurance running. In one, Mo is variously in the lab attached to all manner of monitoring devices, on a treadmill, on a track (alone), running down the street (alone) and, inexplicably, at the bottom of a swimming pool with weights attached to his feet. The value of individual hard work is emphasised throughout. 'That's when you realise you don't need assurance, only endurance,' says the voiceover on one advert. The message of the Nike ad is very clearly: it's you against the world and you don't need anyone else. This is particularly strange, because it's very much not how Farah actually trained, either in the US or in Ethiopia or Kenya, when he was almost always surrounded by teammates and sometimes pacemakers.

Another Nike video ends with the slogan 'Unlimited endurance'. This time the voiceover is Farah himself: 'You could do it, anyone could do it, but the mental part is the hard part.' This is a particularly odd message because it's very clear that nobody has 'unlimited' endurance and it's also obvious that not 'anyone' can win multiple Olympic titles. The notion that anyone can succeed if they just try hard enough is a dangerous one, because it ignores all kinds of structural barriers to success, of which the young runners here face a great many. They might 'train for' winning as much as they like, but without a lucky connection with someone who can get them to the kind of race in Europe they want to compete in, they will never have the chance. It is also unclear that all the runners share the idea that this is all about individual work and dedication. I ask Padam and Anita, who are running the 60km at Sindhupalchok, if it will be strange to compete after nine months of training together at the Initiative. 'No, not strange,' Padam says. 'Training is training and competition is... separate.' But she doesn't look so sure.

I ask Mira to tell me how she got started with running and she talks about competing in road races in Kathmandu alongside the training she was doing for karate at the time. She ran primarily in 5km and 10km races whilst also playing football and volleyball. 'When I got to Kathmandu I was crazy to just play as much sport as I could,' she explains. 'Running seemed like a good option, because you just need a t-shirt and pair of trainers, and then you can just continue...' She entered a half marathon 'by accident', having meant to enter a 10km, and without having done adequate training. 'I didn't know anything,' she says, laughing, 'except just compete like crazy.' She ended up weaving all over the road with 400m remaining before 'finishing my energy completely' and ending up in hospital.

If she entered the half marathon by accident, her trail running debut was even more unexpected. She had joined in with some other runners on the trails around Kathmandu and they had invited her to meet them at the entrance to a park at 6 a.m. on a

Saturday morning. Excited to have someone to train with, she turned up to find people setting up the start line for a 50km trail race. 'I thought, why not? Four or five hours and I'll be finished.' She laughs at the memory. 'But it was raining, and the up and downs in the trail were crazy, and then there was a storm and I wasn't prepared for anything. But I won and I enjoyed it.' As she ran she thought about all the trails she had covered as a child and with the Maoist army. 'As I was moving in the trail I thought, "Wow, this is also sport. *This* is the sport I will change."' It wasn't the sport that would change her. She realised this was the sport she wanted to transform in Nepal.

I am struck by two things as Mira recounts her early running experiences. The first is that when she talks about road running she does so with her hands – this is how she gestures to show how flat a course was, or to indicate that she was weaving backwards and forwards across the road. But when she talks about trail running she can't sit still. She is practically hopping up and down on the chair, her shoulders animated and her gestures expansive. The second thing is that she talks about 'running' on the roads but 'moving' on the trails – trail running, it seems, is more holistic, occupying more of herself. I ask her about the differences between road running and trail running.

'When I move in the trail I feel more confident, and more relaxed and more flexible,' she says. 'When I run on the road I still like to run, but it doesn't feel natural. When I'm on the trail I feel more natural in myself and better. I don't know why.' Even when she was little she preferred to be outside and on the move, in spite of the fact that the expectation was for a girl to remain in the house. She would chop wood, shepherd cattle and carry baskets of rice weighing up to 28kg. 'In the village I was always moving in the hills,' she says. 'I had a friend who was a little older than me and we were always racing to see who would be first to cut grass, who will collect the water most quickly… I don't know if this was exactly running, but I was younger than her and she always won, but I was still trying. You know, never give up.'

She found the daily routine of going to school, cutting grass and collecting water stifling, though, and from a young age she was looking for other opportunities. 'Chances are like leaves on a river,' she says. 'You have to grab them, as they may never come again.' This is a philosophy she has applied to her running, but it was also how she approached the decision to sign up for the Maoist guerrilla army and leave home, in spite of the fact that the only thing she knew about the Maoists at the time was that they provided two meals a day. 'In both you are just finding a way, you know?' she says. Joining the Maoists was an opportunity to leave the village and learn about wider Nepalese society.

'In the Maoist army there were a lot of young friends like me and if you worked hard you could become a leader, step by step,' she says. 'So we listened, and we followed them and learnt sport from them.' There was also a great deal of singing and dancing in the Maoist army, and she still finds the songs popping into her head in races. Her time in the army also opened her eyes to the wider realities of life in Nepal. 'Before I signed up, I knew that my family were struggling and that we worked hard just to eat. But I thought that problem was just with myself and the village. When I went to the Maoist army I found a lot of people who shared my background, whose parents were also like my parents.' She met other young 'brothers' and 'sisters' who had aspirations similar to hers, like joining the Nepalese army or leaving the country. 'You know, there's a lot of dreaming,' she says.

By the time she got to Kathmandu it was with a passion to make something of herself through sport that she tried her hand at lots of different things, with varying success. There were points when she considered going to Malaysia to find work, following a path that many young Nepalis take to precarious work in various places including the Gulf States. It is clear from talking to the young athletes here that running is one strategy amongst many for improving their lives and sometimes – like in Lopsang's case – not the first choice. Anita talks about her brother who works for the Singapore police force having survived a selection process at least as competitive as the one to join the Gurkhas. Professional trail running is one of a number of potential ways of making money that rely on discipline, physicality and the ability to endure.

I ask Mira about the trails in Nepal and about whether she thinks the environment here is particularly good for training, but she keeps returning to the issue of funding within the country. 'In the world the sport is growing amazingly, it's flying. Every week more organisation, more support for athletes, everybody working really hard. There's the world championships, there's Sky, there's UTMB, it's great to see the growth of all these things.' There are still very few races in Nepal, though, and she worries about the sport dying out completely. She has succeeded in organising quite a few local races, but is keen for the government to support trail running more and establish an official association. 'We have a lot of good runners,' she says, 'but we don't have a sport culture yet.'

It is very clear from talking to her that she doesn't see her role as merely representing Nepal at the highest level, as she has already done in the Sky Running world series and at UTMB. She sees her role as building the sport from the ground (or the trail) up, by arranging races and fundraising to support the next generation, even if this is at times detrimental to her own training. It is also clear, though, that she sees trail running as an important way to build connections between people both within Nepal and overseas. When she talks about athletes from the Mira Rai Initiative going to races abroad, as Anita did, she refers to this as a form of 'exchange', emphasising the extent to which running together over long distances can forge connections between people. Her dream for the future is to establish a training centre for Nepalese trail runners in the hills outside Kathmandu and to provide a platform for athletes to get to more international races.

I ask her whether, when she is running, her thoughts are about her more political work or her past in the village. 'What do you think about in particularly hard moments, like in the middle of the night in a long trail race?' I ask. 'I just think about trying to continue, think about how I feel and about eating well, continue up and down, continue to focus on course markings and checkpoints.' Her mind never wanders then? 'No. Enjoying and keep moving, it's very good to do that. Not thinking too much beyond this. Just keep moving however much is possible. Every 15 minutes remembering to drink, simple things like that.'

I am reminded here of what Charlie said about it being important not to dissociate from discomfort, but instead to acknowledge and accept it. Take an interest in it, even, and I am struck by how frequently Mira uses the word 'enjoy', especially in relation to the tougher parts of a long race. It is almost like a mantra, a constant reminder of what all this is supposed to be about. I ask her about Sindhupalchok and what I should expect from the race.

'This is the most technical,' she says, 'up and down.' She reaches high up above her head before plunging her hand down steeply towards the ground. Grinning, she adds, 'It's so hard this race, you'll enjoy it so much. Most of the uphills will be fast walking, then running on the flat and downhill sections. Especially at the end, running through all the rice paddies, it's beautiful.' I ask what she is hoping for the athletes from the Initiative – 60km seems a long way to run at 19 or 20 years old. 'This is mostly to give them an idea and to give them a chance to learn about how to remain positive,' she says. I decide that this is what I will focus on, too. My mantra will be, 'Eat well, move well, enjoy.'

* * *

Our instructions for actually getting to the race are quite cryptic: we will receive a text message on Friday morning telling us where to meet at 11 a.m. and that we will travel to the start points by bus. I take a taxi to the designated meeting place, which turns out to be a bar and music venue. In one corner a faintly hungover-looking guy smokes a cigarette and looks on as we mill around in our brightly coloured gear, collecting our numbers. Jimi, the race organiser, bounds around distributing energy bars and introducing people to each other, and he hands me a big bag of insect repellent to pass around. 'It's worth using this,' he says, 'even if it doesn't do much for the leeches.'

He introduces me to Stina, who works co-ordinating the efforts of the 42 different UN programmes currently working in Nepal and has lived here for 20 years. She's run all the trail races. I explain who I am and what I'm doing.

'This is your *first* ultra?' she queries. 'Why'd you pick this one?!
60km doesn't sound that far,' she says, 'but I'd rather run the
Kathmandu rim 100-miler than this.' I ask why. 'The trails are
about as technical as they get, and the climbs and descents are
incredibly steep. Last year there were three earthquakes during the
race and they had to re-route the finish to include a river crossing
because of a landslide,' she explains. 'That added about four hours.'
I am beginning to regret asking questions about the race. At the
registration desk Jimi is cheerily telling someone whose bank card
isn't working that they have to make sure they pay the entry fee
before the race 'in case you die or get lost forever.' When Lopsang
ambles over to say hi he is wearing a t-shirt that reads, 'In the
footprints of the historic Maoist guerrilla war trails.'

They have, at least, marked the trail with paint as well as
coloured ribbons this year. 'The kids like to take the ribbons,' Stina
explains. 'Or they move them as a joke.' I can imagine these detours
become less funny the more hours you have been running. Tellingly,
everyone at registration who ran the 60km last year is running the
28km this year. We are loaded on to separate buses to travel to the
different start points and I sit with Sher Tharu, who sports a
handlebar moustache and who was second in the race last year. He
is keen to exchange Strava details and shows me the data from his
recent 24-hour run in Delhi, where he covered 190km. 'This
should be relatively easy then,' I comment. 'Oh, no, Delhi was like
this,' he says, indicating with his hand that the course was paper
flat. 'And we just went round and round. Sindhupalchok is more
like this,' he adds, waving his hand dramatically up and down.
'And always searching for markers.'

Although most people have switched from the 60km to the
28km, there is one person who has decided to go the other way.

As the bus is slowly pulling out on to the road, Liam, an American who is living in Kathmandu for a few months whilst interning with the NGO Restless Development, jumps on to the bus through the still open door. This is met with cheers from the others inside as Liam pumps his fist and sinks into the chair across the aisle from me and Sher. 'Man, I wonder if I'm going to regret this,' he says. He's not done a great deal of running in Kathmandu, put off by the traffic and pollution, but he's run a multi-day stage race in Corsica recently so he's a little more prepared than I am for the hills.

Sitting with Liam is Raibat Dahal, who wears a Nepalese army cap and a red Adidas jacket with 'Nepal' emblazoned on the back. He is a clerk in the army now, but was a soldier for many years and is still a very competitive trail runner. We share the food we have with us for the journey – chocolate digestives, an especially spicy Bombay mix and some almonds. I look around for Arjun Rai, who was pointed out to me as the winner of last year's race. He is sprawled across the back seat of the bus, fast asleep. If the evidence I've seen of elite Ethiopian runners the day before a race is anything to go by, this suggests that he will be very difficult to beat.

We stay the night before the race in tents pitched in the grounds of a local primary school, and the local kids don't let Liam and I rest until we've raced the length of their football pitch. After five hours on the bus I try to sprint and almost stumble into the dirt as Liam streaks away for a convincing victory. The kids keep asking him to sing them a song and he inexplicably opts for a rendition of Shaggy's 'It Wasn't Me', which goes down extraordinarily well. As we are chatting on the football pitch Stina walks over and points to the hills in the distance. 'Look,' she says. The clouds have cleared enough to see beyond the lush green slopes to the real mountains behind. They rise improbably white, austere yet sublime in the evening sunlight. Moments later the clouds return, the veil replaced once more so that their appearance feels almost like a mirage.

A local tea house prepare a huge plate of *dal bhat* – rice and lentils – for us. '*Dal bhat* power!' Sher grins. *Dal bhat* is such a staple here that it is sometimes used as a synonym for food more generally – to ask someone, 'Have you eaten?' you say, 'Have you had *dal bhat*?' Fuelled up, we settle down for a night on thin mats on the concrete school floor. Before I go to sleep I remind myself of my mantra for the morning: 'Eat well, move well, enjoy.' I add one more element: do not race. If I want to finish this thing I have a feeling I will need to work with people rather than against them.

The next morning we head down to the local tea house again for breakfast – some spicy fried potatoes, more lentils and a hard-boiled egg – and find that half the town are already up and waiting to see us off. Jimi had warned us that whilst the start time was officially 5.30 a.m., it was likely we would be setting off a bit later than this. Ceremony is important here and with an election coming up there would be speeches from local dignitaries. To get to the start line we have to walk around a row of red plastic chairs that have been put out for local politicians to sit on and several people speak at length as we are given first white then red *khatas* – traditional Tibetan Buddhist prayer scarves.

These kinds of scarves are commonly presented for luck at the outset of a long journey and this is how I've decided to approach the day, rather than seeing it as a race. We also have our foreheads daubed with a vermillion *tika*, made from rice, water and coloured powder, to mark the upcoming Dashain festival. The *tika* has religious significance for a number of groups in Nepal and sits between the eyes at the point of the *Ajna* or sixth chakra, a seat of concealed wisdom. The *tika* is intended to focus energy and increase concentration, and to serve as a medium of personal sanctification. At around 6 a.m., with the scarves safely handed over to an official, the race begins, heading straight down a steep and mud-slick set of stairs.

Sher, Arjun and a couple of others scamper off into the early-morning mist, taking rapid little steps round the switchbacks and seeming to jump down some of the steeper sections. They are followed by Padam and Anita from the Mira Rai Initiative, and I settle into a slightly more tentative rhythm with Liam and a Nepali runner called Prakesh. It would be quite embarrassing – not to mention painful – to come all the way to Nepal only to break an ankle on the first descent. The trail is extremely narrow and very overgrown in places, so you have to place your feet with hope a lot of the time, unable to see exactly what lies beneath the vegetation. On top of this the surface keeps changing – from a reddish mud to big brown leaves starting to mould to firmer ground covered with a greenish moss. The ability to read all these different surfaces is one I've only just started to learn with Will and Lopsang, but I get better at it as I descend and eventually the trail evens out a bit, so that I am able to do something that feels a little more like running.

Liam, Prakesh and I separate and regroup periodically, depending on our descending speed and our ability to spot the trail markers, but our effort is collaborative. We shout to each other if we find a ribbon and we try to warn each other about particularly sketchy patches of trail. At one point Liam gets a bit further away, but I can hear him whooping with joy as the forest thins and we can see the hillside opening out in front of us, the morning mist slowly clearing away. His joy is infectious and I find myself running with a huge grin on my face. At the bottom of the descent we hit a river and I spend quite a while trying to get across with dry feet, thinking about the blisters that will result in a few hours' time if I run in wet shoes.

I finally accomplish this, only to find that after last night's rain the narrow trail up the next hill has become a channel of fast-running water about six inches deep. I am starting to learn that ultra-running is as much about the ability to make these small, cumulative calculations as it is about the ability to keep pushing, and that sometimes the careful calculation proves a waste of time. Liam and Prakesh are now a few minutes ahead, so I set off to catch them up, trying to find a good rhythm, alternating fast walking and running when the trail allows it.

I find that Mira's phrase 'move well' keeps coming back to me. Rather than getting anxious about not being able to run a lot of the more difficult sections, I focus on just covering ground as efficiently as possible, on trying to stay loose and enjoying the feeling of making progress along spectacular trails. Soon I catch up with Liam and Prakesh, and for the next couple of hours the three of us yo-yo back and forth as I push a little harder on the uphills before getting caught again with my cautious descending.

There is very obvious and in some cases quite dramatic evidence of landslides, and the organisers have had to work hard to place markers in a way that keeps the runners as safe as possible, whilst also trying to avoid causing additional erosion. When we're together, Liam, Prakesh and I help each other to navigate these sections. Whilst the course is marked at least every hundred metres, either with ribbon or with a blotch of orange paint on a rock, I find myself missing turnings increasingly frequently and having to retrace my steps, frustrated each time by the loss of energy this represents.

Sections of the trail are lined with beautiful gourd-shaped orange and pink flowers, which look a lot like the trail ribbons, and I have to get quite close to them before I can distinguish between the two. Remaining alert at all times required unlearning something I've seen as a skill in other kinds of races: the art of switching off for periods of time and noticing nothing more than the stitching on the back of an opponent's vest in front of me. Now, each time I allow my mind to wander it costs me several minutes of retracing my steps.

In the first 15km we have dropped from around 1500m above sea level to about 700m before climbing a further 1000m, and this is all before the really big hill, which starts after 30km. I have no idea how I am going to react to this, because in Durham there is no way to train for a hill that continues to go up for more than 10km. Before the climb, though, is another long descent, lasting around 12km. I try to vary my movement as much as possible, visualising the way Lopsang and others descend, with a combination of quick shuffling feet and small jumps and skips.

At the bottom of the descent is a spectacular suspension bridge, with rice paddies rising into the hills on either side. It bounces wildly as I jog across it and when I reach the other side I can't see a marker, so I descend some steps to the road. I know that I am heading towards Jalbire, so I ask a woman who I pass on the road which way to go. She points over another bridge further up the road, so I run a few hundred metres to cross the bridge and start heading up the hill. I find no markers, though, so I decide to retrace my steps. When I get back to her, the woman is adamant that I'm going the wrong way for Jalbire, but I climb the steps back to the swing bridge and there, clear as day, is a big orange arrow pointing left.

It is also pointing uphill, so I wonder if my brain is starting to process information selectively. Jalbire, according to the course elevation profile printed at the bottom of my number, is the lowest point of the race and, sure enough, after a couple of hundred metres of climbing the trail drops down to a village where there is a checkpoint with more rehydration sachets, fruit and packets of vanilla biscuits. I restock and then look up the enormously steep road out of the village. I've already been going for about five hours and, whilst I've covered over half the distance, it seems like I'll be heading uphill for the next couple of hours.

On several occasions on my way up the climb I stop to let groups of women pass. Using a forehead strap they carry enormous baskets of grass or rice and make their way cautiously down the hill in sandals. Mira described doing similar work both as a child and as a member of the insurgency, and it seems obvious that it would represent extremely good training, both for ultra-distance trail running and for working higher up in the mountains. The rehydration sachets we were given at the beginning of the race feature a picture of a mother feeding a baby, a reminder that they are designed to treat diarrhoea-related dehydration, which still affects a lot of people, especially children, in Nepal. I can't help wondering what these women make of me, sweating my way up this hill with my little backpack of water and rehydration salts, thousands of miles from home, for no discernible reason at all.

As I head through one of the villages I'm surprised to see Sher walking back down towards me with a wry smile on his face, holding up his scratched and bleeding hands in a gesture of surrender. 'I fell over many times,' he tells me, 'and now I have a problem with my leg.' I try to cajole him into continuing with me, but the leaders must be an hour or more ahead by now and he was here to contend for the win. 'You go,' he says, 'just keep moving.' I have fallen once so far – my right leg shooting out in front of me on the red mud – and my wrist is a bit sore from catching myself. It occurs to me that my approach to risk is a privileged one. I don't need to be in the top three in this race, so there is no need for me to end up sprawled in the dirt multiple times.

This is not to say that there aren't near misses, and some sections of the trail are so steep I more or less have to lower myself down with my hands. I have learnt by now to be especially careful on the red earth, which is known as *rato mato*. Lopsang warned Will and I that it was almost impossible to get a decent grip on it, and he taught us a rhyme to remind us to be careful. As I run, I repeat to myself, '*rato mato chiplo bato*' – red earth, slippery path.

I am actually much happier heading uphill, even when the trail is made of a seemingly endless series of foot-high stone steps. There is a particularly steep section a couple of kilometres out of Jalbire and it is so steep that a couple of times I am forced to sit down and gather myself. Perhaps luckily the steps are also crawling with ants, which makes it unwise to sit for long in split shorts. I am just beginning to wonder if I will ever make it to the top when a little shop appears like a mirage to my left, a tall fridge gleaming implausibly in its corner. I have a soggy emergency 1000 rupee note in my bag and I decide that this is close enough to an emergency.

I buy a cola called My Cool Cool and it is genuinely the best thing I've ever tasted in my life. Firstly, it's flat, so I can drink it in about three seconds. Secondly, it's freezing cold. And finally, it's made with some kind of artificial sweetener that tricks my brain into thinking I have been supercharged. I thank the little boy in the shop and get back to the stairs with a new spring in my step, which lasts at least 50m. Whilst I've not managed to exactly run the whole way I've already been going for two hours longer than my previous longest run and I'm surprised to find that I go through patches – even after seven hours or so on the move – of feeling really good. I wonder if these peaks and troughs of energy and emotion will continue to get bigger as I get closer to the finish.

On the little elevation profile chart on my number the checkpoint at Yanglakot is right at the top of the big climb, so every now and then I ask people I pass on the trail where Yanglakot is, hoping to determine from their reactions roughly how far away it is. Most of them gesture in a vaguely 'just up there' kind of way that gives me hope. Given that at the last checkpoint I was told that the leaders were 'about ten minutes' ahead, though, I am prepared to take any information with a large pinch of rehydration salts.

The problem with the elevation chart printed on my number is that Yanglakot is not at the top of the hill at all and after a brief stop at the checkpoint I am on the move again, munching vanilla biscuits. Strangely, I am feeling great, in spite of the hill having no end in sight. Not euphoric or anything, but decidedly like I've got several more hours in me if I need them. This is just as well, of course, but for now I'm enjoying the light drizzle that has started to fall and the fact that I'm still running – slowly, but running nonetheless – up the slightly less precipitous incline. All around me are vast walls of green forest obscured only by small patches of mist, with tiers of rice paddies shelfing off downwards.

The section after the climb looks, at least from the printed profile, like the most theoretically runnable part of the course and it feels like I might actually be able to use it to make up some time. It doesn't take long, though, to be disabused of this notion. The trail *is* wider and less steep than anything I have encountered so far, but it is made of big paving stones stacked vertically, so that they stick up at strange and painful angles, making running downhill on them with quads in the state mine are in extremely unpleasant.

The extended downhill running also makes the straps of my running bag dig into my shoulders, causing a strange tingling sensation in my arms that gets worse until my right arm is more or less completely numb. It briefly occurs to me that this is one of the symptoms of a heart attack, but after a few minutes of running with the bag first in one hand then the other the blood returns to my arms and I can wear it again. I'm amazed to find that almost as soon as the trail starts going downhill I wish it would go back up again, even after just finishing a 12km ascent.

Finally, mercifully, the trail does flatten off and when it does it is absolutely stunning. I am in a valley surrounded on all sides by tiered rice paddies and the trail skirts around their edges, so that you have to be very careful not to step into the water. The sun has come out, and the only sound is birdsong and the gentle trickle of the irrigation systems feeding the rice. Once again, I find my mood absolutely transformed. I've been moving for almost 10 hours and yet I find myself in the curious position of wanting to lengthen the time it takes to get to the finish rather than shorten it, to extend the experience as much as possible. I make sure I take in the rice paddies, and appreciate the ingenuity of the stone paving that hems them in and which I have the privilege of running on.

The last kilometre of the race involves running down yet more steps, my knees protesting more and more all the time, and now I do want this to end. Finally, the trail winds between (and sometimes through) tightly packed stone houses, until finally there is an archway with two orange ribbons tied to it. I stagger through and realise that I have – to no fanfare at all, after 10 hours – finished. Eventually Jimi notices, and jogs over and gives me a high five, exclaiming, 'We have another finisher!' to the two guys manning the final checkpoint. Beyond them, in a large grassy courtyard, they are already handing out the prizes for the 60km race.

I put my hands on my knees and say, 'Please tell me the prize for first non-Nepali is a cold beer,' and in no time I'm sitting with an enormous bottle of cold Everest beer, which seems appropriate. Padam and Anita have been finished for well over an hour already, having run the whole route together. They've been relaxing in a pool by the river and look like they could probably run the whole thing again. They say they kept themselves going by thinking of their parents and Mira, their coach, and that when things got really hard they turned to motivational songs.

I barely have time to drink the beer before we need to get on the bus back to Kathmandu – it's either that or stay in Sindhupalchok for the night and I have commitments the next day. On the way back to the bus we have to cross a narrow wooden bridge suspended over a deep gorge and gale force winds whip around it, causing it to shake violently. Full of postrace euphoria people jump up and down on it, and stop to take videos of the Nepalese flag flapping in the wind.

This jubilant mood continues on to the bus where we are crammed close together. I've not had a chance to change and I'm still in my shorts and soggy, mud-soaked running shoes, but I don't really care. I ask Padam, who finished so far ahead of me, how she was able to run so strongly. She tells me that she's from the hills, where life involves going 'up and down' every day, and she talks about the agricultural work, mostly carrying large bundles of grass, that she had to do before school. 'So if we can participate in races we can do it,' she says simply.

In between banging his head on the window as the bus lurches along the mountain road, Will tells me that this is an explanation many people give. Gopal, for instance, told him about running for three hours to school and back every day with two friends, mostly on the kinds of *sano bato* or narrow mountain paths that technical trail races demand mastery of. Running on these trails from a very young age means he never developed a fear of downhill running.

There is a sense that this might be changing, as there was in Mexico. 'I interviewed an older runner, who had also been in the Nepalese army,' Will says, 'and he said it has always been the case that people had to be extremely fit just to live their day-to-day lives. But then he did this' – and here Will mimed revving a motorbike engine. Apparently people do far less walking now than they did in the past and there is also a sense that young people are increasingly relying on foreign work rather than subsistence agriculture.

That said, the vast majority of competitive trail runners Will knows come from the hill regions. Arjun, who won the men's 60km race, comes from the Solukhumbu, where many climbing Sherpas also grew up. He worked as a trekking porter for several years at high altitude and credits this with building the strength to compete in trail races. He entered his first race on a whim, his 'only training' being carrying heavy loads over high-altitude passes for months on end, and found he was very good at it.

In spite of the advantages of a hard rural upbringing (in terms of becoming a formidable trail runner at least), the runners here are aware of trying to compete internationally from a disadvantaged position. Whilst earlier I explored how many ultra-runners crave simplicity and an escape from technology, Will has found that his Nepalese friends feel that lack of access to these things is a barrier to competing internationally. 'Trail running is a much more technical sport than road running,' is how Will puts it. 'So whilst for Nepali hill people the fitness adaptations gained from their rural lives suit them, especially for up-and-down trail running, road running is actually more accessible to them economically.'

He goes on, 'So I've met very few Nepali runners who would say to me something like, "Oh, we're just going to run in sandals and eat rice." The almost universal ambition of serious trail runners in Nepal is to compete at the global level against relatively affluent athletes, who benefit from the use of ever-advancing technology, and scientific training and recovery methods.' He has therefore found the runners to be extremely keen to embrace anything from foam rollers to GPS watches, which are seen as an especially big advantage in Nepalese races.

'As you'll have gathered by now, it's the pleasure of the village children to take the course-marker ribbons to put on their bikes and in their hair,' he says, 'so a GPS file is especially useful.' In some races GPS files are available, but if you don't have a watch you're just handed a list of place names where the checkpoints are. He tells me of one friend who recently missed a checkpoint whilst leading a race and trekked back to find it. An Israeli runner with a GPS watch was in second place, and he asked him which way it was to the checkpoint, but the Israeli just ignored him. 'I guess they thought, "I've got lucky here, I want to win,"' Will says, 'but my friend was pretty angry about it.'

By the time we approach Kathmandu the immediate postrace raucousness has subsided and we're starting to get hungry. I'm also starting to wonder if I'm going to be able to get out from my cramped position on the bus when it eventually stops. There has been a lot of discussion – amongst the runners and with the driver – about where to stop for something to eat and eventually it has been decided that we should make a detour to a very specific fried fish restaurant.

I stumble inside with my bag and ask if there's somewhere I can get changed out of cold, wet kit. There's no toilet, so I am ushered through a little wooden door into the back, where a huge fire burns to cook the small fish the restaurant is known for. I try to get changed without getting too covered in ash, interrupted briefly by a man coming down some stairs at the back. Random English men clearly don't get changed in the kitchen that often, because as soon as he sees me he quickly retreats up the stairs backwards.

I make my way back into the restaurant to a large plate of fried fish on a communal plastic table and a big bottle of chilled Gorkha beer. Somebody is playing the same Gurkha song I heard in the training camp on my phone and I ask Will to translate some of it for me. One line is, 'I'm going far away, don't cry mother, standing in the doorway/I will return and remember you.' For many of the male runners here this has a clear relevance, but the song seems to resonate with Padam and Anita as well, who can't (at the moment at least) join the Gurkhas.

In seeking a future as a trail runner they, too, must travel far from home and there is clearly a strong desire to represent Nepal. The notion of 'Nepal the Brave' is especially important to the so-called 'martial races', the people from the hills who were originally recruited by the British to be Gurkhas and who also happen to be the best trail runners. Most of the runners look to the government to provide more support for trail running, but at the moment it seems like private sponsorship is the most likely route to races abroad.

I am also struck by some of the similarities to the runners I knew in Ethiopia, for whom running was only one potential way of going abroad and 'changing their lives', as they put it. However, trail running represents a particularly attractive way of doing this when compared with some of the other options, like domestic work in the Gulf States or labouring on dangerous construction sites, both of which are also physically exhausting kinds of work. It is also interesting that athletes like Arjun started as trekking porters, much like many of the high-altitude climbing Sherpas, before moving into trail running, and I am now going to meet some of those people who make their living in the high mountains.

10

CHOMOLUNGMA

Climbing Mount Everest is the feat to which every other act of endurance seems to be compared, from riding the Tour de France to running a four-minute mile – an 8850m yardstick against which everything else is stacked. For instance, musing on the possibility of Eliud Kipchoge breaking two hours at the Berlin marathon following his success at the Ineos 1.59 Challenge, *New Yorker* writer Ed Caesar wrote, 'It would be like the first person to summit Everest with supplementary oxygen doing it without gas three years later. Mallory, Norgay, Messner rolled into one.' In popular speech we use 'the Mount Everest of' as a superlative for all kinds of things.

As I walk the crowded streets of Kathmandu's Thamel district it seems like everything is named after Everest. A huge poster proclaims, 'Touch the Himalaya at Everest Hotel', above a sign for Everest Salon, whilst across the road people queue at Everest Bank. Back in 1999 anthropologist Sherry Ortner explained that the mountain is called Chomolungma in Sherpa (hence the title of this chapter) and Sagarmatha in Nepali, and predicted that, 'These names will increasingly be used in public discourse as the century progresses.' This has not, thus far at least, proven to be the case.

Mountain climbing is perhaps the most literary of all sports – climbers tend to be well educated and articulate, and they are fond of recalling their exploits. Single expeditions can therefore often produce multiple book-length accounts from the perspectives of different expedition members. In spite of this, we still know relatively little about the climbing Sherpas, whose work keeps the Himalayan mountaineering industry going, and many of the accounts we do have feature problematic racial stereotyping and assumptions about their lives in the mountains.

In early accounts, Sherpas who were hired as porters and guides are described as 'childish' and undisciplined. Charles Bruce, leader of the 1922 Everest Expedition, for instance, describes them as 'irresponsible' and 'given to drinking at any opportunity'. Gradually, as the Westerners involved in the expeditions realised how capable they were, this characterisation of the Sherpas as lazy and lacking discipline becomes combined with the idea that they are physically superior.

Over a hundred years ago for example, Francis Younghusband, as chairman of the Mount Everest Committee, wrote that 'right on the spot' of the villages in the Solu Khumbu, there 'must be dozens of men who could, as far as bodily fitness goes, reach the summit any year they liked. Yet the fact remains that they don't [...] They have not the spirit.' The idea that the Sherpas lacked the 'spirit' has clearly been disproven thousands of times since Younghusband wrote this, but the idea of Sherpa physical superiority remains.

Sherpas' ability to carry heavy loads 'has to be seen to be believed' wrote English mountaineer Hugh Ruttledge in 1933. 'Who would believe,' wrote Swiss mountaineer Gabriel Chevalley 20 years later, 'to see them trotting off, that they were each carrying 60kg? It's stupefying.' In 1978, the great Italian mountaineer Reinhold Messner – the first climber to make a solo ascent of Mount Everest – wrote, 'For my money – the Sherpas are supermen.' And more recently still, a CNN article from 2016 entitled 'The biological secrets that make Sherpas superhuman mountaineers' refers to 'the ease with which they deal with the physical challenges' of scaling the world's tallest mountains.

Edmund Hillary's account of the first ascent of Everest with Sherpa Tenzing Norgay is very complimentary. He writes, for instance, of Tenzing forging a particularly difficult route in spite of being up to his hips in snow. 'Almost lying against the steep slope, he drove himself onwards, ploughing a track directly upwards,' he writes. 'Even following his steps was hard work.' He is also honest about the uneven division of the more domestic aspects of the expedition. 'I jabbed the uncomplaining Tenzing in the ribs,' he writes of waking at one of the highest camps on the mountain, 'murmured a few words about the cooker, and then snuggled back into the depths of my sleeping bag.'

Tenzing had 20 years of mountaineering experience by the time he summited Everest, including on notoriously technical mountains like Nanda Devi. After his ascent he dedicated himself to training the next generation of climbing Sherpas, founding a training centre in Darjeeling. The Swiss, who provided funding and resources, insisted he go on their own mountaineering courses at the Swiss Foundation. In his second book, *After Everest*, Tenzing notes diplomatically that, 'It may seem strange to readers that [I] should have to go to school again to learn the fact of mountaineering,' in spite of all this experience. The assumption, clearly, was that Tenzing relied on pure strength rather than technical ability, an assumption that is clearly erroneous if you read his and Hillary's accounts. This notion that the physical aspect of climbing at these altitudes comes naturally to Sherpas persists even today.

Do climbing Sherpas find climbing Mount Everest easy? What is it like to work on the world's highest mountains and be responsible for keeping people safe? What qualities do Sherpa climbers themselves think are most important for performing prodigious feats of endurance? These were the questions I want to answer by interviewing climbers in their time between expeditions in Kathmandu.

I conduct most of my interviews in a first-floor café in the Boudhha area of the city, named for the enormous spherical *stupa,* which is said to entomb the bones of Kassapa Buddha and which is a site of pilgrimage for Tibetan Buddhists. The café is called Café Epic and is run by Sharmila Tamang, photos of whom adorn a back wall covered in plastic ivy. Each of the photos depict her standing at the top of an 8000m peak, with Everest in pride of place at the top and Annapurna, considered the most difficult (and dangerous) of the 8000m peaks, to the right. Sharmila holds the distinction of being the first woman from the Tamang ethnic group to climb four of the 8000m peaks and her ambition is to climb all 14, a feat which has been accomplished by only a handful of women.

In the course of our many meetings in the café, the conversation returns again and again to the question of funding. For Sharmila to complete her project, the cost of permits alone would be in the region of $200,000. The process of raising the money, of travelling to Europe to pitch the idea and herself to potential sponsors and marketing executives, is as draining as the high-altitude climbing itself. She is desperate to find the money, though, both to increase the profile of Tamang women and to raise awareness about human trafficking. 'This is a problem that affects every village,' she tells me, 'almost every family. So many young girls go to the Gulf States to work every year.'

She wants to show women from the region where she grew up that you don't have to go abroad to make something of yourself. 'The best way to motivate people is to do things in the mountains,' she says. A bookshelf on one wall holds a variety of aspirational volumes, including Barack Obama's *Dreams from My Father* in English and a book about Jack Ma, the Chinese founder of Alibaba, in Nepali. These are interspersed with training manuals like *Rock Climber* and maps of the Himalaya. Whilst I am able to talk to quite a few climbing Sherpas, she laments the fact that many of them are on Manaslu at the moment, poised for a push to the summit. 'If you were here after that there would be a lot of drinking in the café,' she laughs, pointing to a large fridge stocked with Gorkha and Everest beer.

The reason so many people are on Manaslu is because of a debate about where, exactly, the true summit of the mountain lies. When Sharmila and I are joined by a Sherpa climber called Mingma, the conversation about this drifts between English and Nepali, so I find it slightly difficult to follow. It seems, though, that the mountaineering statistician Eberhard Jurgalski, who runs an exhaustive and labyrinthine website called 8000ers, published a PDF of the summit profile of Manaslu which showed that many climbers who thought they had reached the top – including some who have climbed all 14 8000ers – had actually taken their summit photos at one of the 'fore-summits'. In some cases this meant they had been mere metres from the true summit of the mountain, which still seemed to be the subject of some debate.

Living with uncertainty and an incomplete record are not in the nature of the kind of people who spend years of their lives, and hundreds of thousands of dollars, climbing the 14 highest mountains on the planet, so this information has compelled several expeditions back to Manaslu. It is not until I am at the airport waiting for my flight back that the full cost of the expedition hits home, though. I check my phone to see a message from Sharmila. 'Avalanche on Manaslu,' it says. 'My friend Anup has died, another five injured.'

The question of what exactly it is that drives people to climb these mountains is one that is taken up in Sherry Ortner's *Life and Death on Mount Everest*. 'I was stunned by the extravagant purposelessness of the deaths of these young men,' she writes of her early fieldwork amongst Sherpas and foreign mountaineers. 'I became extremely hostile to mountaineering. Words like "lunacy" and "bizarre" were sprinkled through early drafts of some of the chapters that appear in this book.' It is hard not to react in this way, too, when I hear about unnecessary deaths caused simply by a new technique of measuring the relative heights of mountain peaks.

I interview Angdorje, who was actually supposed to be on Manaslu and only cancelled the expedition he was supposed to lead a few days beforehand. This was because of a disagreement he had with his client, who wanted to pay him 50% of his fee upfront and 50% *if* they reached the summit. 'Some people demand that,' he says, before adding, in an understated way, 'but life is important.' The client, it turns out, was prepared to pay for his own insurance, but not for insurance for Angdorje. There are clearly still foreign climbers who place a very different value on their own lives and those of the Sherpas in whose trust they place them.

One of the main things that comes through clearly in the conversations that I have with climbing Sherpas is that, for them, endurance is absolutely not about pushing through intense discomfort and refusing to accept defeat. That, in fact, is how you get killed. All of the climbing guides I met had rules about who they would and wouldn't work for, with some ruling out entire nationalities on the basis that they would refuse to turn around even if the situation was desperate. They were wary of men (and it was almost always men) who were so proud that they would rather die in the attempt and would often take a guide with them rather than turn back.

When I ask Angdorje how he keeps himself going through difficult situations, we need Sharmila's help to translate. Interestingly, whenever this kind of question gets translated into Nepali they always use the English word 'motivate' rather than a Nepali or Sherpa equivalent. I wonder if there is any significance to this – if you are climbing as your job perhaps it becomes less a question of motivation and willpower, and more one of making decisions in a professional way. He tells me about one particularly challenging expedition on Kanchenjunga, when he had to carry one of the clients, who was suffering from severe altitude sickness, all the way back to base camp from near the summit. He checked that the client was OK, had a hot drink, then turned round again and went all the way back up, later escorting another client to the summit.

His answer to the question of how he keeps himself going is that when he feels exhausted he thinks of his family and, in particular, of his daughter. 'I think about the fact I don't have any other option,' he adds. In thinking of his family, Angdorje is also reminding himself that he needs to make careful calculations to weigh the risk and reward of getting to the summit in particularly challenging conditions. For climbing Sherpas summits are important – the first thing most of the people I interview tell me is how many times they have stood on the summit of Everest and other major peaks. There is almost always a large financial bonus for reaching the summit. Considerations here are more about the endurance of life itself than the ability to continue to push on in spite of everything.

Getting to the summit for a climbing guide, though, is almost entirely dependent upon their client, who they are usually paired up with one-to-one at some point during an expedition. The success, and the safety, of an expedition, often come down to the relationships of trust and respect that Sherpas are able to build with clients in a short space of time, and it is this aspect of their work that people return to again and again in our conversations. When a client is struggling on the mountain and their oxygen-starved brain is incapable of rational thought, the Sherpas need to be able to look them in the eye and say, 'We've got to go down, *now*,' and be listened to.

Lakpa has been on 10 Everest expeditions and summited six times. To describe him as 'barrel-chested' would be an understatement; he is built like a large fridge-freezer. When I ask him whether he thinks Sherpas are naturally stronger than people from other places he answers with an immediate one-word 'Yes' and a laugh. For him, the most important factor in a successful expedition, though, is not strength, but teamwork. 'You have to create discussion,' he says. 'I insist on eating together, discussing everything openly, working on relationships.' This final point – explicitly cultivating the right kinds of relationships for successful work, seems crucial. 'Everyone is a long way from home,' he reminds me. 'Everyone misses their family. So it is better to work together.'

Lakpa frequently erupts into rasping laughter as we talk. I ask him if he is surprised by how many people want to come to climb the 8000m peaks. 'Yeah, yeah,' he says. 'I don't know why. They come because they have money or because they want to be the first. The first from their country, their region, their club, their office...' He laughs, then adds between chuckles, 'They want to be the first dentist from their town.'

This is not to say that he doesn't understand the pull of the mountains, though. I ask him what significance Everest has for him personally. 'It's professional,' he begins. 'It's my job, and I take it seriously.' Then he adds, 'But it is also an adventure. I like to just be in the mountains. There is more peace. It's quiet. There is good energy – positive energy.' He gestures to the busy street outside, to the motorbikes squeezing round people, before adding, 'You forget all your stress at home. You have some meditations, you know? You feel younger. It's like Shangri-La, it returns you to the age you were when you were last there.' Finally he grabs his belly before pointing to the beer fridge. 'Anyway if I stay in Kathmandu too long I drink too much beer with my friends,' he laughs.

Lakpa has had quite a remarkable career, which began when he was a teenager and joined a rescue team looking for a Canadian woman who had got lost above Dhaulagiri base camp. Like many of the trail runners I met in Nepal, he was strong because his first ambition was to be selected for the Gurkhas. 'I broke the trail for hours on the way up,' he says, but he struggled on the way down due to his lack of experience. A friend, who worked in the mountains, sent him for mountaineering training with the Nepal Mountaineering Association and he started with the basic course before working his way up.

He is keen to emphasise the importance of luck to a successful career in the mountains, too. When it came to taking the advanced course with the Mountaineering Association, there were three outstanding candidates for one place and the instructor made them roll dice to decide who would get it. Since that moment

Lakpa has felt that luck is on his side. After a high-altitude climbing career that spans four decades, he thinks that this is more important now than ever. The mountain is becoming increasingly dangerous, the opportunities for summit attempts becoming ever narrower.

'The snow and ice are melting rapidly,' he explains. 'There are only two or maybe three windows in the season when you can summit safely, and these are getting shorter and more difficult to predict.' In order to work within these constraints, which he sees as clearly created by climate change, he calls for, 'More control, more organisation and more regulation' of the mountain. As he speaks I begin to see the famous photo taken by Nirmal Purja that circulates on social media of the snaking line of climbers on the Hillary Step 'queuing' for the summit in a different light. Whilst many commentators decry the absurdity of this and idealise the notion of the lone climber standing on the summit, Lakpa and many of the other Sherpas I talk to see this kind of co-ordinated effort as a necessary safety precaution.

Sharmila has kindly agreed to introduce me to the president of the Nepal Mountaineering Association, Mr Rudra Singh Tamang, who shares similar concerns to those raised by Lakpa. We meet at the outdoor courtyard of a brand new glass and steel shopping mall, and chat with soft musak playing in the background. Like many of the other people I meet whose lives have been spent working in the mountains, Rudra started as a porter carrying equipment between camps at the age of just 13, before working his way up to running his own trekking company.

Since he started working in the mountains in 1977, Rudra has seen first hand the extent to which the industry has transformed people's lives. 'When I was 13 I worked at Annapurna Base Camp,' he says. 'I thought, "This is heaven! But very cold." And life for people living nearby was difficult. I wanted to do something about this for Nepal.' He therefore sees the promotion of mountaineering in Nepal as a balancing act of boosting the local economy whilst also protecting the environment. 'The mountain environment is broken right now,' he says, 'with pollution and so many things. Climate change is a very big problem in Nepal, but it is not Nepal's fault. We are not controlling heavy industry.'

He has introduced rules to clear up on Everest and everyone who goes to Base Camp must now bring back 10 to 15kg of rubbish themselves, a rule that has resulted in the disposal of over six tonnes of waste so far. One of the main functions of the Nepal Mountaineering Association is to provide accredited mountaineering courses to train climbing Sherpas, with the aim being to make the mountains as safe as possible. To that end, the association also controls the provision of permits to climb any peak above 5800m. Rudra spends a lot of his time lobbying the Nepalese government, who are ultimately responsible, to tighten the rules for foreigners who want to climb the very high mountains. The permits for the 8000m peaks are an important source of revenue for the government, but allowing inexperienced climbers to attempt Everest is dangerous for the Sherpas.

'The problem,' he says, 'is that inexperienced people join the expeditions. They think, "I can buy the people. They can carry me." That concept is bad.' Climate change has made climbing more dangerous, both for the clients and for the Sherpas who guide them. His suggestion is that anyone who wants to climb an 8000m peak should have to first climb a 6000m and then a 7000m mountain in preparation, a stipulation that seems extremely sensible, but which in his experience some foreigners don't have the patience for.

Given the virtual monopoly on working in the mountains that Sherpas now have, it is amazing to reflect that a century ago there was no culture of mountain climbing in the region at all. Lakpa is keen to remind me that when the first survey expeditions to Everest arrived from Darjeeling and tried to recruit Sherpa porters and climbers, they found it very difficult. 'Before then no Sherpa climbed the mountains, because they respected the mountains as a God. They thought they were making it dirty and so there would be disasters.' He holds his hands up as if to acknowledge that disasters are, in fact, a fairly regular occurrence. 'So actually in our culture there was no climbing. We respect the mountain as a God, a female God.'

Not surprisingly, then, early accounts of climbing in the Himalaya document a certain reluctance from Sherpa porters. As Sherry Ortner notes in her book, 'They usually had to be made to go on.' Gradually, though, they 'had to learn to be willing to go on (even, to desire to go on) without anyone making them do it; that is, to acquire self-discipline under the constant shadow of death.' There are other people living at high-altitude in the Himalayas, including Tibetans and other Nepali ethnic groups, such as the Gurung and Thakali. Precisely why the Sherpa, and not other ethnic groups in the region, were so motivated to use mountain climbing to both literally and figuratively elevate themselves is a question that is difficult to answer.

One explanation is that it was an opportunity for social mobility for a group of people who didn't often have that. In Sherpa society there was quite a clear divide between 'big people', who owned more land and livestock, and 'small people', who didn't. In a place with no paved roads and no wheeled vehicles, where almost all transportation was on foot and almost everything was carried on people's backs, most people were used to carrying heavy loads up steep slopes from a young age. However, one of the most significant ways in which the 'big people' differentiated themselves from the 'small people' was that they didn't carry loads.

Whilst what we might call the middle class might have carried their own water and other loads, the 'small' people would have spent their time and energy carrying for those more powerful than themselves. They were therefore incredibly strong by necessity, not because of some genetic predisposition. With expeditions to the big mountains, there was suddenly an opportunity to make good money from something the 'smallest' people in Sherpa society were most skilled in. Overnight, strength, and the ability to persevere through the most challenging circumstances, had the power to transform the social hierarchy in Sherpa society. Tenzing Norgay went from tending sheep with a lifetime of farmwork ahead of him to speaking to audiences of dignitaries all over the world.

Even today, moving up the hierarchy from porter to climbing guide is often a process of having to carry less. When he told me his life story, for instance, Mingma Sherpa spoke of first working as a porter and then a cook. 'I worked on support cooking – kitchen staff – for eight years,' he said. 'I had to carry a lot of stuff!' he adds, making an expansive gesture. 'So then I thought, hey Mingma, the guides and the climbing Sherpas, they don't carry much. I want to change my job! So then I went to the Nepal Mountaineering Association to do some training.' Being promoted to climbing Sherpa was a major triumph – it was better paid, more prestigious and, crucially, meant less carrying.

This is not to say, of course, that it does not still involve enormous amounts of physical work, including the highly skilled process of fixing ropes high up the mountain. This often involves multiple trips up and down from camp whilst the client climbers rest, in camps that have often been laboriously constructed before they even arrive in Kathmandu. I ask whether this work of fixing ropes and setting up camps is harder than actually guiding clients up the mountain.

'Oh yeah, much harder. Because it's blue ice you have to work with, you're carrying all the ropes, you're carrying ice screws, everything. Then you have to carry all the tents, food, oxygen canisters, the clients' personal stuff. It's very hard. But in spring there are so many Sherpa guides there that they can share man power.' Working together, again, is crucial to making all of this possible and all the guides I spoke to expressed a preference for working in pairs or teams to working alone. In fact, as one of them put it, 'If you see a single figure in the distance you know it's not a Sherpa.'

For Mingma, the ideal number of people to have in Base Camp is around 200 – enough for it to feel like a community or a small village. Being there is about work, but also about catching up with friends, having a good time and building team spirit, which is seen as vitally important for reaching the summit safely. These attempts don't always work, though. In 2013, for example, one of the main companies organising Everest expeditions, Seven Summits Treks, set up a bar and outdoor theatre, and organised dance nights, which were relished by the Sherpas, but more or less ignored by clients who preferred to relax in solitude or were merely too exhausted.

Often the hardest part of an expedition is the descent, because the clients are often weak and disorientated, and the Sherpa guides have to look after them whilst also carrying equipment down the mountain from the various camps en route. If oxygen canisters or other debris are left, other expedition guides will photograph it and they will be fined, and it is also important for them to leave as little trace on the mountain as possible. It can clearly be extremely challenging to escort struggling clients down whilst wrestling with all this gear.

'There was one time,' Mingma laughs, 'when it took five of us a whole night to get one guy down. He was bending down and trying to pick things from the snow, talking about beautiful flowers. He kept trying to take off his summit suit. Some people start singing, living in a dream.' He reminds me that this can happen to Sherpas too, even those with a lot of experience of the high mountains. He is able to laugh about this, but these situations must be incredibly difficult to manage when you're close to your own mental and physical limits.

One of the things that strikes me about the guides I meet is their openness to pursuing opportunities to learn and travel beyond Nepal. In Mingma's case, this meant saying yes to an offer to spend the winters running a small guesthouse or *repose* in the French Alps. He had been involved in an avalanche on the sixth highest mountain in the world, Cho Oyu, and had been carried 400 or 500m and then buried in the snow. 'I was quite injured,' is how he puts it. 'Unconscious for 25 minutes.' A concerned former client named Patricia – suddenly aware, perhaps, of the fragility of life – got in touch to ask him if he'd like to go to France. 'She said, "Oh, you've never been anywhere, you should come,"' he says and in spite of knowing very little about what he would be doing (and with very limited French) he agreed.

He laughs about the initial problems he had securing his French work permit. 'They asked me why I wanted to go to France and I said, "Oh, to travel. To have fun." They said, "This is a work permit," so there was a bit of a misunderstanding.' He had to go back for a second interview, where he gave them the answers they wanted to hear, and then travelled to France, where the *repose* turned out to be reachable only on foot, 25km through deep snow. 'The first time took me four hours with snow shoes,' he laughs, 'with everyone passing us, whoosh, on skis!' So the next year he went back three weeks early and 'learnt with the babies how to put on skis.' Now he goes back every year and skis the 25km to work and back each day. 'Everything goes well now,' he sums up, contentedly. 'Yeah.'

The interviews I was able to conduct in Kathmandu gave me an insight into the Nepalese mountaineering industry, but not the depth of understanding I would have gained from actual fieldwork. Luckily for me, though, it turns out there is a Korean anthropologist named Young Hoon Oh who has recently completed research on climbing expeditions. Over the course of two years his research included climbing Everest three times – once in the conventional way, once in the harder autumn season and once without oxygen. In the course of his fieldwork he led two expeditions and acted as an instructor-guide on a further two, climbing as an expedition member on many more, including a dead body recovery mission. Two fatal accidents occurred on expeditions of which he was a part and in total five of his climbing acquaintances died whilst he was doing research.

If I thought it was difficult to balance training alongside some of the best runners in the world with doing anthropological research in Ethiopia, this pales in comparison to Young Hoon's work. By the end of his fieldwork he found he was sometimes able to conduct long conversations with Sherpa climbers at the final camp before the summit of Everest. He notes in his dissertation, though, that during expeditions his mind was often occupied entirely by mountaineering issues 'such as, "How to condition myself today for tomorrow's climb?", "[Should I] climb tomorrow or not?" "What if I die?" and so on.'

When Young Hoon and I speak on Zoom it is late evening in Seoul and I am pleased to see his office is as strewn with books and papers as mine is. I tell him that I am intrigued by the lives of Sherpa climbers and what seems to make them uniquely suited to work in the mountains. 'From the biological angle there has been a lot of research,' he begins, 'but people generally agree that Tibetan highlanders have some genetic adaptations to the environment. This is not a simple process, but it is to do with the size of the lungs and the efficiency of oxygen transmission and so on.'

This sounds familiar to me given my work on Ethiopian running – lots of theorising about genetic or altitude-derived advantage, but no definitive conclusions. 'What is interesting,' Young Hoon goes on, 'is that this is true of all Tibetan highlanders, not just Sherpas. But you should know that it is Sherpas only, not other Tibetan highlanders, not different ethnic groups, that are working in the mountains, right?'

He is keen to emphasise then, that the monopoly the Sherpas have on climbing in the high mountains is down to 'the cultural stuff' as he puts it. He continues, 'You should know as well that I've known Sherpas who have suffered with the high elevations. Not every Sherpa climber is very, very strong. It is not that.' I am reminded of some of the interviews I conducted with climbing Sherpas in Kathmandu, who often recounted similar struggles on their first climbs in the really high mountains: the same headaches, dizziness and disorientation that everybody else encounters.

In fact, the way they talk about working in the mountains is strikingly similar to the way many Ethiopian runners spoke of 'adapting' to world class marathon training. Nuru Sherpa spoke about working on the smaller 6000m and 7000m mountains, before eventually graduating to working on Everest and other 8000m peaks. Of Everest he recalled his progress. 'First camp one, then camp two, camp three, South Col. Finally I was on top of the world,' he said. 'I thought if we work hard step by step we will get success.' After reflecting, he added, 'In any kind of work, if we work hard step by step.'

In Ethiopia, in Amharic, the phrase that was used was '*kes ba kes enkulal begru yihedal*,' which literally means 'step by step an egg walks on its feet.' Complaints about slow progress or lack of fitness were often countered simply with '*kes ba kes*' and a shrug. A patient attitude amongst the Sherpas is even more important: over-extending yourself in the mountains can easily be fatal. 'One slogan I like best,' Aang Sherpa told me, 'is first safety, then success.' This is a long way from the hard-charging language of mind-over-matter nothing is impossible. It also sells less well than the message of things like Nirmal Purja's Netflix documentary on his 14 peaks challenge. 'Giving up is not in the blood,' Purja says. 'The biggest strength I have is I have no fear.' These are not sentiments that the Sherpas I spoke to, who had many relatives relying on the money they made in the mountains, would identify with.

'It's interesting to go back to very early writing about Sherpas and climbing,' Young Hoon goes on. 'Back in 1907 there was a Norwegian expedition to Kabru, in North East India. A report on the climb was published in English in the *Alpine Journal* a year later and this was the first reference to Sherpas in a climbing context. The main thing it notes is that the Sherpas are "cheerful".' I am struck by this word, because I am halfway through Ernest

Shackleton's account of the disastrous *Endurance* expedition, where the word 'cheerful' is used to describe men in the most trying conditions – in an almost hopeless situation, frostbitten, eating dog food after being forced to shoot the sled dogs, but somehow still 'cheerful'.

This is not a uniquely Sherpa characteristic, clearly, but one that Young Hoon thinks stands up after his two years of observation. 'For me the interesting thing is how much a personal characteristic can become a cultural characteristic.' There is a risk here of making exactly the same sort of problematic generalisations that are made about genetics in relation to these kinds of cultural forms, but for Young Hoon it still makes sense to try to trace these things carefully. He is also dismissive of attempts to put a cheerful disposition and an ability to endure down to Buddhist teachings about the acceptance of suffering and disassociation from pain, pointing out that whilst the Sherpas he knew were Buddhist, they came from a region with no monastery and no formal Buddhist teaching. 'So my theory,' he says, 'is that it is not because of Buddhist teaching, but rather Buddhist teaching is a result of their collective ways of living together.'

Emphasising the importance of social relationships and working together is something people living in mountainous village environments would have known from a very young age. 'Culturally,' Young Hoon goes on, 'people have developed the characteristics not to disclose, or to ignore or neglect, those harsh and challenging aspects of their lives.' Rather, they have tended to 'emphasise the good, meritorious and happy moments of their lives.' Whilst Sherpa climbers do suffer, and they experience traumatic events and their colleagues (and clients) die, they 'hardly mention those things amongst themselves.' In fact, he adds, 'in

Sherpa dialects there are very few words that refer to negative concepts such as sadness, sorrow, failure and pain.'

Young Hoon describes the attitude towards pain and tiredness that the Sherpas he lived and worked alongside had as a kind of 'unliving'. He talks about a 15-year-old boy named Sanae who had injured his ankle during a period of time spent away, herding sheep on winter pastureland. He joined him for a five-hour trip up into the hills to supply food to a village, and noticed the way the Sanae worked to disguise his limp and to avoid any outward display of pain.

Whilst he was initially tempted to see this as a sign of male bravado or adolescent shyness, he came to realise that no Sherpas really ever talked about pain, and that there was no Sherpa verb equivalent to our word for 'ache'. Sanae's disguised limping, in Young Hoon's interpretation, was not 'an attempt to show off, but was a by-product of an actual attempt not to immerse [himself] in or "live" the pain.' Similarly, climbing Sherpas rarely if ever mentioned tiredness or showed concern for the weariness of others. This was not a sign of lack of care, but rather an attempt to focus, instead, on the celebration of more positive values.

Young-Hoon lived and worked mainly with Sherpas from the Makalu region and he emphasises that his conclusions might have been different had he worked with Sherpa climbers from Sindhupalchok or Khumbu regions, as mine would have been in Ethiopia had I worked with Oromo runners rather than those from the Amhara region. For Makalu Sherpas it was primarily strength – usually measured in the number of 8000m summits climbed – that was valued above all else. 'Being strong' is a great source of collective self-esteem and a way of setting themselves apart from other groups, and strength in the mountains is seen as inextricably linked to strength in performing the day-to-day village chores that make up mountain life.

There is a certain degree of bravado that comes with this. Locally brewed liquor called *cchang* is also seen as a great source of strength and when Young Hoon told Sherpa friends of his plan to climb Everest without oxygen, for example, he was told to remember to 'bring *chhang* to Camp 4!' to share with the other expedition members. The notion of strength emphasised here, though, isn't just about blocking out pain and pushing on in spite of everything, it is also about maintaining a cheerful outlook and a sense of teamwork, which are seen as a vital part of being strong and as characteristics particular to the Sherpa.

As Rudra from the Nepal Mountaineering Association put it to me, 'Nepalese climbers are always happy, they make other people happy and they have to very strongly preserve their heart to each other.' Everyone understands that this requires a lot of effort, but a big part of enduring in the mountains, then, is about having heart for other people.

11

ENDURING IN A CHANGING CLIMATE

Towards the end of our interview I tell Lewis Pugh, the UN's Patron of the Oceans, that I'm thinking of making the final chapter of my book about endurance and climate change. He sighs loudly. 'But it's the most important thing,' he says, shaking his head. 'It's like David Attenborough, he'll do a whole series about the Antarctic and then it's only right at the end that he'll talk about how it's changing.' This chapter begins with an apology to Lewis, but also with the acknowledgement that the changing climate has come up unprompted in a great many of the interviews and conversations I've had for this book.

For Jacob Adkin, the trail runner I ran with earlier in the book, the Covid lockdowns were 'eye-opening' because for the first time in years he stayed in the Lake District rather than flying to Europe to race. 'I did a whole load of fell races I'd always wanted to do,' he said, 'and that led me to just really appreciate being in the environment you're in.' Rather than flying back and forth to races he now has a van so he can drive down and stay in Europe for the summer. Andy Berry, who helped me train for Lakes in a Day, had made a similar decision. 'I don't want to be jetting off to Europe three or four times a year to run a race when there are a lot of amazing things to do in Britain,' is how he put it. 'I just came back down from Torridon in North West Scotland and – holy shit! – what a place.'

Whilst many people who spend significant amounts of time outdoors are making decisions like this, there are also a lot of people like Lewis making explicit connections between their own endurance and climate change advocacy. We speak an hour before he is due to travel to the Munich Security Conference to appear alongside the likes of Bill Gates and Ursula von der Leyen, and to talk about the distinction between 'bravery' and 'courage'. I'm a bit nervous, less because of the high profile he has than because of some of the challenges he has accomplished. As well as swimming the length of the English Channel (some 350 miles compared to the 21-mile crossing), he has completed extreme cold water swims at the North Pole and in Antarctica. For some reason I decide to mention that I've been reading Ernest Shackleton's account of the *Endurance* expedition and been struck by how often 'cheerfulness' is mentioned, but it seems that isn't quite how he would characterise his experiences.

'There's a big difference between being a climbing Sherpa or those polar expeditions and actually swimming across the North Pole,' he says. 'Yes there's significant danger there, but no human had ever swam in anything close to those water temperatures. I wasn't sure at all of whether I would come back alive.' Salt water doesn't freeze at zero, but at precisely -1.8 degrees Celsius. For every fraction of a degree below zero, there are material changes to the water: it becomes denser, closer to solid ice. And every fraction of a degree has an 'enormous impact on your body'.

It takes a long time to sail from New Zealand to the South Pole, starting at 40 degrees south and going to 50, 60, 70 degrees with no sign of land. There's a lot of time to think and to entertain reasons for backing out, but eventually you reach vast white cliffs. On first glance they almost resemble Dover, but he describes it as 'a wholly unnerving place'. Before Lewis swam in the Ross Sea of Antarctica, his wife Antoinette walked the perimeter of the boat, where the air temperature was -27 degrees Celsius, checking for leopard seals. As the slushy water broke against the edge of the boat it froze in mid-air before crumbling back into the sea.

Normally Lewis can estimate the speed of the wind using the Beaufort scale just by looking at the movement of the water. Here, though, where the water is denser, you have howling gales but a completely flat sea. 'On these journeys these silly thoughts come into your mind,' he says. 'I remember getting ready to start that swim and the thought that came to my mind was, "If I drowned now, how long is it going to take my frozen corpse to sink 4.5km?" So certainly I wouldn't regard anything cheerful [as] happening there.'

Point taken, I think. Not cheerful. 'At that point you have to have the courage to decide to go on,' he continues. 'I felt so strongly about it, having spent seven summers in the Arctic, every year seeing the ice get thinner and thinner, less and less. I've seen what is happening and I believe this is the defining issue of our generation.' He speaks with utter conviction and it's easy to see why the UN would want him to lead the push to protect ocean environments. On his website there is a statement that reads, 'It is the moments that challenge us the most that define us.' I ask him if he sees an explicit connection between the kind of decisive moment he experienced on the edge of the boat in the Ross Sea and the decision that humanity now faces about the climate.

'Absolutely,' he says, which is why he always times his big swims to happen alongside global conferences, where he has the opportunity to speak about these issues. He gives the example of his 76-mile swim across the Red Sea, timed to coincide with the COP27 conference in Sharm el-Sheikh in November 2022. 'We've already heated the planet by about 1.2 degrees since the pre-industrial age,' he says. 'If we get to 1.5 we will lose about 70% of the world's coral and at the moment we're on track for 2.7 degrees.' It is clear how important to him it is that people share his alarm about this. 'It's not like a forest,' he goes on. 'If you have a big spike in water temperature you can lose a coral reef in a week. Can you imagine a big spike in temperature and suddenly we lose the New Forest? So I'm trying to do the swims to shine a light in places of the world which most people are just not seeing.'

His advocacy work can demand a lot of travelling, something which he admits 'doesn't sit comfortably' with him. He justifies this with the example of securing a protected area in Antarctica, which forms part of an effort to protect 30% of the world's oceans by 2030. In the end the deal came down to the support of China and Russia, and whilst Joe Biden negotiated with the Chinese it was Lewis who was given responsibility for persuading the Russians, along with their former ice hockey player turned politician Viacheslav Fetisov. Understandably, this involved a lot of shuttling between Washington and Moscow, as well as the swim he did to draw attention to the region. 'I get lambasted by some people on the left wing of the environmental movement,' he says, 'but that swim, and the work which myself and Slava [Viacheslav] did, led to the creation of the largest protected area in the world. You can do a lot virtually, but you can't persuade the Russians to think about the Ross Sea on Zoom.'

There seems to be a very clear symbolic value to doing incredibly challenging and risky things, and this has enough power to influence geopolitics in significant ways. But Lewis sees as much value in giving people the opportunity to connect to their surroundings in a more everyday way. 'We can't expect people to want to protect the environment if they don't have a connection with it,' he says, 'but when you run in the mountains, or you cycle through a wilderness area, or you hike through an area or you swim down a river, you connect with nature. Most people have never even been to a wilderness area.' He qualifies this by noting that even the 'natural' places people do seek to escape to in the UK – like Dartmoor or the Lake District – are heavily shaped by human activity. He was astonished when the last rights to wild camping in England were taken away recently and he is shocked by what we've allowed to happen to our rivers.

'I work with 196 countries as a UN ambassador and the one country that has completely smashed their rivers is the UK,' he says. His ancestors grew up on the River Wye and he remembers his mother taking him to see where she used to fish for salmon with her father. Now, though, chicken farms pour raw animal sewage into the river along with other waste and nothing is done to stop it. 'The Welsh Government blames Westminster, and Westminster blames the Welsh Government, and they blame the Environment Agency who say they don't have the funding to do the protection and monitoring properly, and the farmers say "Why are we being blamed when we're operating within the law?" and the consumer says, "We're in a cost of living crisis and we need cheap chicken." So everyone is pointing their finger at someone else.'

He has his head in his hands by this point. 'I have to put my hand up and say we're actually destroying the life support system,' he says. 'The rivers are the veins of the country and we're destroying them.' Part of the lobbying work he does around this is to push for rights of way along rivers and the coastline, which would allow people to bear witness to what was happening, to make the connections by moving through the space. This is something that was also clearly important to ultra-runner Jasmin Paris, who I interviewed in chapter 5. 'Because you're moving through these beautiful places all the time, you're seeing first-hand the effects of what is happening,' is how she puts it. In returning to run in the Alps every year she can see the way the glaciers are changing in a really immediate and visual way.

There is also a sense in which moving through these places whilst also pushing your own limits makes this connection more visceral. Ultra-runner Damian Hall, who I talked to in chapter 5, too says, 'We have the heightened emotions within us, but you also feel the terrain and the weather more keenly. When you're really raw and vulnerable the weather is everything and the terrain is everything. You're like, "Oh it's a bit of road – aaah!" and you're sort of internally crying or really crying. Or you kick a rock or something and you feel that so intensely.'

Lewis's work echoes the kind of politically motivated running that is still practised by the Hopi to deliver important environmental messages, where the message is lent weight by the effort and suffering that goes into its delivery. As Jasmin puts it, 'If you're the sort of person that wants to push your limits and boundaries, even if that's not in terms of competing necessarily, then you tend to be pretty driven. And if you combine that with a love of the environment that makes you want to act, that's essentially what takes you to climate activism.'

This also seems to be a part of what the Green Runners are trying to do with their advocacy work. What started as a UK-based WhatsApp group for runners interested in lessening their personal environmental impact has since grown into a running club with over 1000 members and an increasing commitment to advocacy. For many of them this is a somewhat reluctant activism. Damian, for instance, has pledged not to run any UTMB races whilst they have a high-carbon headline sponsor (the car manufacturer Dacia), which wasn't an easy decision to make.

Whilst in the past endurance challenges were often marked with the flags of nation states, symbolic of imperial rivalries played out at poles and on mountain tops, Damian unfurls an Extinction Rebellion flag made by his children when he finishes events like the Spine Race or the Tor des Géants. 'Obviously this works better when you do well in the race,' he laughs when he tells me about the Tor de Géants in 2023. 'Last year I was 12th, and I finished at 2 a.m. and got the flag out. There were three people there half asleep going, "Yeah, nice one." This year, though, I was fourth and it was a better time of day and there was a media team there and we were able to capture it a bit better.' Media team or not, it can be hard to deliver a coherent message after three days and nights of running. 'I think I just said something like, "We're all part of the problem, but I'm really tired now and I need to lie down,"' he laughs, 'so I sort of messed up.'

He says he feels a sense of duty to use his running to spread awareness or 'keep making a fuss' as he puts it. Like Lewis, he is occasionally accused of hypocrisy and virtue signalling, even though almost all his travel to races these days is by train. It is a major aim of the Green Runners to support each other in reducing their own carbon footprints, but he thinks the emphasis on the individual is misplaced. 'It's corporations and governments who are really causing the huge damage,' he says.

Sports psychologists tend to say it's important to know your 'why' when you're preparing for an event. 'You've got to think,' Damian says, 'about what your values are and what's going to motivate you 48 hours into a race when it's dark and you're hurting.' For both Damian and Jasmin, in these moments their thoughts turn first to their children. 'I think parents have a bit of a cheat code there,' Damian says. 'It's very emotive to think of your kids and the fact that you're trying to do it for them, even though they probably don't care.' The climate emergency is secondary to this, but intimately linked. 'I have a bit of a platform from running,' he says, 'and I want to use it. I'm a father and I just think what are our kids going to think of us, and their kids? They're going to look back on us as selfish and lazy and much worse than that I think.'

The Green Runners have organised their own events to bring out the connection between endurance running and the environment, such as the Climate Relay, which involved a large number of people passing a baton over 1652 miles from Ben Nevis to Big Ben. But there are others creating their own independent adventures to do this. I heard about Rosie Watson from a colleague. Rosie came up with the idea of the New Story Run towards the end of her time at Leeds University. She had wanted to do a long self-supported run for a long time, but wasn't sure she could justify it to herself. Tying the adventure to an attempt to 'change the narrative' on climate change transformed her attempt to run across Europe from what might have seemed a frivolous jaunt to a project with a purpose. Her intention was to run from the UK to Mongolia, without a support network or sponsorship – a kind of DIY experiment in endurance and communication.

By the time we speak we do so via Zoom during a break from her new job as sustainability manager for the running brand Inov-8. She tells me she departed from the Lake District on 17 August 2019 and stayed with friends for the first few days before arriving, by ferry, in Holland. 'The first night it felt like the real deal was when I arrived in the Netherlands,' she recalls, 'because you're not supposed to wild camp. I was running along the cycle path and there was all this scrubby woodland, so I waited until there was no-one in sight then sprinted off into the undergrowth and out of sight,' she laughs. 'So it was like the opposite of Instagram camping where you're looking for somewhere with a nice sunrise or something. You wait until it's dark to camp then get going again when it gets light.'

Rosie's project was twinned with a bike ride by her boyfriend at the time, Mike Elm, which followed a slightly different route but had the same goal of gathering stories from people involved in climate advocacy. To a certain extent, their routes were planned to involve meeting particular people and hearing their stories, but both found that doing this in the form of an endurance challenge shaped their encounters in profound ways. Journeying in this way is slow, it promotes a kind of careful noticing of surroundings and it seems to make connecting with people easier.

If you turn up on a bike or on foot after covering thousands of kilometres and shivered through freezing nights in a tent, people react in unexpected ways. 'We have this idea that people are afraid of strangers,' Mike says, 'but the overwhelming feeling was of people being interested and helpful. If I'd driven up in a car it would have been very different, but on a bike people are immediately like, "OK, this is interesting, what's happening here?"' Again, it is the vulnerability that is created that leads to connections being made.

Mike also found being on his bike and moving slowly from village to village allowed him to hear a more complete story than, for instance, a journalist dropping into one place. For a long time he followed the Vjosa river, which flows from the Pindos mountains in Greece and through the canyons, plains and forest of Albania. The river is the last undammed, fully wild river in Europe, and has recently become part of the first wild river national park, protected by a number of NGOs and the outdoor company Patagonia.

When Mike was cycling through, though, he stayed in villages which were still scheduled to be flooded as part of a proposed dam project. He saw numerous protests at the roadside and heard people's concerns about the flooding of land that held their ancestors bones, as well as the alternative solutions people proposed, like solar panels on the rooftops of homes. By following the river it was possible to hear the story all the way down and draw connections between the concerns that people had at different points. 'The thing about doing this as a kind of endurance challenge is that you're forced to see everything, not just the parts you're supposed to see,' he says. 'You see all the dead parts and ruined parts and ugly parts as well, so you understand the context much better.'

For Rosie the main motivation for her run was to tell a new kind of story about the climate crisis. 'It was mainly a communication project and the running really helped with that communication because it was such a weird thing to do. I was able to amplify the messages.' She says she wasn't actually trying to promote active travel in particular – the main reason she ran was because she loves running. In this sense it was in the spirit of the British environmental philosopher and adventurer Kate Rawles, who, in 2006, cycled 4553 miles from Texas to Alaska, exploring climate change as she went, and documented it in the book *The Carbon Cycle: Crossing the Great Divide*. The idea that activism should take whichever form makes you feel most alive really resonated with Rosie.

Looking back there are some ways in which she regrets tying the run so clearly to climate activism, because it turned what was supposed to be an adventure into a project and then something that almost resembled a job. 'It kind of took off in terms of people getting into it and the media around it, and I did kind of see it as like a job by the end,' she says. Having recently finished university she felt she needed 'something to show' for running 4800km across Europe, a way to prove this was an intellectual as well as a physical endeavour. 'At the beginning I had this vision of collecting all these positive stories,' she says. 'But there was a point near the end of the run where I just felt like everything I was writing about was just a tiny drop in the ocean compared to the scale of the crisis. Then I also had this pressure that I'd created this whole journey that was about positivity and I felt I couldn't really express the gloom of it all...'

This combined with the tiredness from running and pushing so far eventually led to Rosie completely burning out by the end of the run and needing to take a long time to recover from the fatigue. When we speak, she's still only able to run short distances and still trying to work out exactly what happened. 'Energy is just very strange,' she says. 'I can't really tell you anything useful about it, because I don't really understand it myself.' What has happened since the end of the run is that she's recalibrated her relationship with both endurance sport and climate activism.

'The best piece of advice I've been given is to do the right thing, because it's a good thing to do,' she says, 'not because you think it's going to be linked to a specific change. If you think, "I'm going to do this and it's going to make this happen" then as soon as there's any doubt about whether or not that impact is measurable or whether you're going to see it, or whether it actually is working, then you're just demoralised. Whereas if you do the thing just because it's the right thing to do, it's a much healthier way of looking at it.'

The same is true with her goals around running. 'If I was just doing it because I felt like I had to reach Mongolia at all costs, which was the original goal, then it would be a failure, because I didn't. I barely even got half-way. But I realised I wasn't doing it for that, I was doing it because of the adventure which happens in the tiny day-to-day moments of bumping into someone and having a chat with them on their doorstep. That's the important stuff actually; the overall big goal isn't. The goal is the thing that keeps you moving in a certain direction, but it's not the actual adventure.'

Her experience with fatigue over the years following the New Story Run has taught her how important the tiny interactions that sustain us are. The little kids who would materialise alongside her wherever she went, jumping for high-fives. Or the old Albanian woman who stopped her on the trail who, unable to speak English, grabbed one of her hands, kissed it, and then waved her on her way. 'I was so full of beans after that,' she says, 'because she was just trying to encourage me and was just happy that I was running along. Those interactions only last a few seconds, but they can completely transform your day.'

Alongside attempts to harness endurance sport to the climate movement there have been other attempts to explicitly connect moving more with social change. A great example of this is GoodGym, which was started in London by Ivo Gormley. I met Ivo when he came out to Ethiopia to visit Ed Stevens, a mutual friend of ours, and he explained the concept to me in very simple terms. He asked me to think about how much energy – both human and machine – was wasted in gyms when it could be put to use getting things done and increasing human connection. GoodGym organise 'missions' where members get together and do things like run a few miles to a patch of ground that needs to be cleared, do some digging together and run back again, or where people run to the house of a lonely older person to keep them company for an hour.

I finally catch up with Ivo seven years after we met in Ethiopia. 'My theory about this is that meaningful collective activity is extraordinarily good for everything,' is how he puts it. This theory has been backed up by a large-scale study of GoodGym conducted by the London School of Economics, which found clear evidence that feelings of wellbeing, belonging and connection improved with participation in GoodGym whilst loneliness and mental distress diminished.

For Ivo it seems important for human connection that there is some level of challenge involved, but for it to be truly 'meaningful' requires something useful to be achieved as well. 'In terms of physical activity increasing social connection that's something Ed actually says out loud,' he says, referring to our friend in Ethiopia. 'He'll suggest something that sounds terrible to me, like walking 30km to my parents' house in Norfolk from King's Lynn Station. We got there at 11 o'clock at night, had a kebab and started walking. And I said, "This is a terrible idea" and he said, "Yeah, but we'll *remember it*!" and he was right.' Ivo sees this as an example of 'fake purpose', of just doing something 'pointless and exciting' and he would put running an ultra-marathon in this category as well.

'Where wellbeing is highest,' he goes on, 'is where something is built in like a grape harvest where everyone is brought together and you have fun stomping on grapes but you're also more involved with food production.' Active transport is an important starting point – getting where you need to go on foot or by bike – and it's even better if you can actually do something socially useful that also requires physical exertion. 'That could be hunting a deer if that's relevant to you,' he says, 'or it could be delivering some medicine to an isolated older person.'

Emily Tupper spent over a year with GoodGym in order to write her PhD thesis on movement-based volunteering. She writes that this emphasis on harnessing and using energy rather than allowing it to go to waste is more than a mere metaphor 'at a time in climate history where people are increasingly aware of the impacts and effects of their own bodies on the world.' GoodGym's activities are not just about putting energy to use in new ways, though, they are also about building connection and trust between people. Emily noticed that the people who met regularly for 'missions' would then feel far more comfortable asking their GoodGym friends for help in their own lives, for example.

Crucially, GoodGym focuses on a 'fine-grain' approach to volunteering, fitting it into people's lives through regular, low-impact activities, and there is a lot of emphasis on keeping things as fun and interesting as possible. Emily found that many people stressed the pleasurable and social aspects of volunteering in a way that complicates the idea that volunteering should be a form of sacrifice.

If we are looking for useful parallels to our evolutionary past it might make more sense to look to things like GoodGym, and cycle and run commuting (when I interviewed Tao for chapter 3 he emphasised that his bike was a form of transport for many years before he saw cycling as a sport), than to paleo diets and barefoot running shoes. For people like the Rarámuri and the Hadza, endurance practices are thoroughly embedded in day-to-day life and necessity, in the process of getting from A to B, and in the building of social lives.

In reality, though, what we see is a coming together of different ideas about what it means to endure. When I spoke to him in 2016 Ivo was working out how to respond to feedback from GoodGym participants that they wanted ways of quantifying their 'good deeds' and rewards for reaching particular milestones, which is what ended up being implemented and which Ivo sees as key to their success. GoodGym is 'purposefully non-competitive and trying to tap into a different motivation than being the fastest, and making it more about your connection and your contribution,' he says. 'But people are still very, very interested in that kind of comparative stuff, so everything you do is recognised – you don't opt into that, you actively need to opt out of having a record of all the great stuff you've done.' This demonstrates that the urge to compare and compete and quantify can co-exist with an emphasis on social connection and helping others.

As the geographer John Bale notes, running, in particular, encourages the perspective of 'front space', which is 'primarily visual and perceived as the future. It is sacred space, towards the horizon, yet to be reached.' It is perhaps therefore natural to wonder about where all this is heading. At the Conference on Enhancement in London I heard various predictions. Lord Stone of Blackheath, for instance, imagined a utopian scenario where we embrace technologies in a way that leads to human self-actualisation, away from competition and towards making the planet a more beautiful place. But I also heard people say that we need to enhance ourselves in order to compete with the machines that we are creating.

At the moment, it feels as if we are at a bit of a crossroads between the embrace of capitalism and technology on the one hand (with the Ironman take-over of UTMB, for example) and a search for other kinds of meaning in endurance sport. My hunch, though, is that the pendulum will continue to swing between an interest in extreme forms of tracking and a desire to be free from these things, between 'barefoot' and 'super shoes', and between seeing endurance sport as ritual and as the chase for records.

Through the process of tracing endurance practices around the world, I have come to see more similarities than differences. As I was running around a four-mile loop in Durham for the seventh time one day in July, it suddenly occurred to me that the backyard ultra format that is so compelling to people today has striking similarities to Rarámuri *rarájipari* races. I realised I'd chatted to someone different on every loop so far, the conversations gradually becoming less inhibited as we became more fatigued. I mentioned this to Stuart, who organises these informal backyard events every few months and he laughed. 'Yeah, that's the main reason I organise them,' he said. 'This is a much better way of connecting with friends than going to the pub or something.'

This is just one more of a great many examples of people emphasising the social importance of moving together, whether on an overnight bike ride in the Scottish borders or on the top of Everest. It seems clear that endurance is imbued with a range of meanings – from the practical to the spiritual, the personal to the activist – and this can only be a good thing, but as we put one foot down in front of the other it's worth thinking about where we want to direct these vast quantities of human energy.

BIBLIOGRAPHY

1. Threlkeld in the Rain

Kelly, D. (2017). 'Running Towards My Father: On Marathons, Perfection and the Impossibility of Intimacy'. (https://lithub.com/running-towards-my-father/)

Turner, V. (1969). *The Ritual Process: Structure and Anti-Structure*. Routledge.

Till, C. (2014). 'Exercise as Labour: Quantified Self and the Transformation of Exercise into Labour'. *Societies* 4(3): 446–62.

Beckett, S. (1983). *Worstward Ho!* Calder and Boyars.

Freeman, L. (2023). *Running*. Duke University Press.

Crawley, M. (2020). *Out of Thin Air: Running Wisdom and Magic from Above the Clouds in Ethiopia*. Bloomsbury.

Tsing, A. (2004). *Friction: An Ethnography of Global Connection*. Princeton University Press.

Rusert, B. (2017). *Fugitive Science: Empiricism and Freedom in Early African American Culture*. NYU Press.

Magness, S. (2014). *The Science of Running: How to Find your Limit and Train to Maximise your Performance*. Origin Press.

McDougall, C. (2009). *Born to Run*. Profile Books.

Algeo, M. (2017). *Pedestrianism: When Watching People Walk Was America's Favourite Spectator Sport*. Chicago Review Press.

Martin, C. (1994). *Dance Marathons: Performing American Culture in the 1920s and 1930s*. University Press of Mississippi.

Westaway, J. (2015). 'Rituals of Extinction: Manhunting Games in the British Outdoor Movement, 1890-1914' (https://vimeo.com/159778798)

Finnegan, W. (2016). *Barbarian Days: A Surfing Life*. Corsair.

2. Rarámuri, Mexico

McDougall, C. (2009). *Born to Run*. Profile Books.

Lumholtz, C. (1905). *Unknown Mexico*. Macmillan.

Lieberman, D. et al (2020). 'Running in Tarahumara (Rarámuri) Culture: Persistence Hunting, Footracing, Dancing, Work, and the Fallacy of the Athletic Savage.' *Current Anthropology* 61(3).

Geertz, C. (1973). 'Deep Play: Notes on the Balinese Cockfight' in Geertz, C. *The Interpretation of Cultures*. Basic Books.

Bentham, J. (2022/1802). *Theory of Legislation*. Legare Street Press.

Noveck, D. (2007). 'Playing Places: Imagining the Indigenous in the Rarámuri Indian Violin'. PhD thesis, University of Chicago.

3. The Art of Tracking

Bale, J. (2004). *Running Cultures: Racing in Time and Space*. Routledge.

Haraway, D. (2006). Interview with Kunzru in Geertsema, H. *Cyborg: Myth or Reality?* Zygon, 41(2).

Schull, N. D. (2014). *Addiction by Design: Machine Gambling in Las Vegas*. Princeton University Press.

Till, C. (2014). 'Exercise as Labour: Quantified Self and the Transformation of Exercise into Labour'. *Societies* 4(3): 446-462.

Schull, N. D. (2016). 'Data for Life: Wearable Technology and the Design of Self-Care'. *Biosocieties* 11(3).

Noble, S. (2018). *Algorithms of Oppression: How Search Engines Reinforce Racism*. NYU Press.

4. To the Sun

McNeil, W. (1997). *Keeping Together in Time: Dance and Drill in Human History*. Harvard University Press.

Radcliffe-Brown, A.R (1922). *The Andaman Islanders*. Cambridge University Press.

Durkheim, E. (1912). *The Elementary Forms of Religious Life*. Oxford University Press.

Turner, V. (1966). *The Ritual Process: Structure and Anti-Structure*. Aldine Transaction.

Shepherd, N. (2011). *The Living Mountain*. Canongate.

5. Lakes in a Day

Ingold, T. (2011). *Being Alive: Essays on Movement, Knowledge and Description*. Routledge.

Rigauer, B. (1981). *Sport and Work*. Columbia University Press.

Caillois, R. (1958). *Man, Play and Games*. University of Illinois Press.

Atkinson, M. (2011). 'Fell Running and Voluptuous Panic: On Caillois and Post-Sport Physical Culture'. *American Journal of Play* 4(1).

Lyng, S. (2004). Edgework: *The Sociology of Risk Taking*. Routledge.

Vonnegut, K. (1952). *Player Piano*. Charles Scribner's Sons.

6. Technology and the Elephant in the Room

Schumacher, Y. (2014). 'The Athlete Biological Passport: Haematology in Sports'. *Lancet Haematology* 1(1).

Sottas, P. et al. (2011). 'The Athlete Biological Passport'. *Clinical Chemistry* 57(7).

Kelner, M. (2017). 'Inside the Doping Hotspot of Ethiopia: Dodgy Testing and EPO Over the Counter'. *Guardian* 04/08/2017.

Ikaika Sports (2023). 'Experts on Kipruto: Facts say he is not cheating. ABP should protect clean athletes, not bully them'. Press release 17 May 2023.

Banfi, G. (2011). 'Limits and Pitfalls of the Athlete's Biological Passport'. *Clin Chem Lab Med* 49(9).

Enhanced (2024). https://enhanced.org

Guttman, A. (2004). *From Ritual to Record: The Nature of Modern Sports.* Columbia University Press.

7. Enduring Social Media

Gershon, I. (2017). *Down and Out in the New Economy.* University of Chicago Press.

Latour, B. (1992). *Aramis, or the Love of Technology.* Harvard University Press.

Toffler, A. (1980). *The Third Wave.* Bantam.

Marwick, A. (2015). *Status Update: Celebrity, Publicity and Branding in the Social Media Age.* Yale University Press.

8. On Running and Being Human

Bramble, D. and Lieberman, D. (2004). 'Endurance Running and the Evolution of Homo'. *Nature* 432.

Newman, R. (1970). 'Why is Man Such a Sweaty and Thirsty Naked Animal: A Speculative Review'. *Human Biology* 42(1).

McDougall, C. (2009). *Born to Run.* Profile Books.

Dyreson, M. (2004). 'The Foot Runners Conquer Mexico and Texas: Endurance Racing, "Indigenismo" and Nationalism'. *Journal of Sports History* 31(1).

Brownell, S. (2008). *The 1904 Anthropology Days and Olympic Games: Sport, Race and American Imperialism.* University of Nebraska Press.

Lavi, N. et al. (2024). 'Rewild Your Inner Hunter Gatherer: How an Idea About Our Ancestral Condition is Recruited into Popular Debate in Britain and Ireland'. *Current Anthropology* 65(1)

Longman, D. et al. (2023). 'Human Energetic Stress Associated with Upregulation of Spatial Cognition'. *American Journal of Biological Anthropology* 182(1).

Liebenberg, L. (1990). *The Art of Tracking, The Origin of Science*. David Phillip.

Guenther, M. (2017). '"…the eyes are no longer wild. You have taken the Kudu into your mind": The Supererogatory Aspect of San Hunting'. *The South African Archaeological Bulletin* 72(205).

Nabokov, P. (1987). *Indian Running: Native American History and Tradition*. Ancient City Press.

Gilbert, M. (2018). *Hopi Runners: Crossing the Terrain Between Indian and American*. University Press of Kansas.

10. Chomolungma

Ortner, S. (1999). *Life and Death on Mount Everest: Sherpas and Himalayan Mountaineering*. Princeton University Press.

Hillary, E. (2003). *High Adventure*. Bloomsbury.

Norgay, T. (1977). *After Everest: An Autobiography*. Allen and Unwin.

Oh, Y.H. (2016). 'Sherpa Intercultural Experiences in Himalayan Mountaineering: A Pragmatic Phenomenological Perspective'. PhD thesis, University of California Riverside.

Adams, V. (1996). *Tigers of the Snow and Other Virtual Sherpas: An Ethnography of Himalayan Encounters*. Princeton University Press.

11. Enduring in a Changing Climate

Shackleton, E. (2015). *South: The Endurance Expedition*. Penguin Classics.

Rawls, K. (2012). *The Carbon Cycle: Crossing the Great Divide*. Two Ravens Press.

GoodGym (2024). https://www.goodgym.org

Tupper, E. (2022). 'Moving Together: An Ethnography of Movement Volunteering.' PhD thesis, Durham University.

Bale, J. (2004). *Running Cultures: Racing in Time and Space*. Routledge.

ACKNOWLEDGEMENTS

This book spans continents and academic disciplines and, in general, involved biting off at least as much as I could chew. There are therefore quite a few people to thank.

In Mexico, I would like to thank Silvino Cubesare for his generous hospitality, which included night drives through the Canyons, organising dances, and extreme patience with my many questions about Rarámuri running. Many thanks also to Mickey Mahaffey for his assistance with translation, for sharing his stories and for being a great travel companion.

In Nepal, I thank Will Lloyd for giving me a window into his fascinating PhD project. I also thank Lopsang Tamang for showing us some amazing trails, and everyone at the Mira Rai Initiative for their time and hospitality. Thanks also to Jimi Oostrum from UNICEF for organising a spectacular race. Sharmila Lama was extremely generous in sharing her mountaineering journey and introducing me to lots of people who work in the mountains.

Thank you to all of my interviewees in the UK and US for making the time to speak to me. There are too many of you to name everyone, but thank you in particular to Tao Geoghegan Hart for making the time to speak to me during injury rehab, to Jasmin Paris for making time whilst training for her record-breaking Barkley Marathons and to Charlie Spedding for allowing me to spend time with one of my all-time running heroes.

I am grateful to Duncan Stibbard-Hawkes for our conversations on running and evolutionary theory, and for careful readings of draft chapters. Other generous readers include Steve Bell, Leo Hopkinson, Ben Hildred, Tom Carter and Tom Yarrow, as well as the participants in the International Network of Sport Anthropologists' feedback sessions. Thank you to my dad for being my most enthusiastic and supportive reader, and for finding the mistakes in my Spanish transcription. I also benefitted from many conversations with colleagues in the anthropology department at Durham, particularly Kate Hampshire and Tom Widger.

At Bloomsbury I would like to thank my editors Charlotte Croft and Sarah Skipper for their support and expertise, and for helping me keep the overly-academic language in check. Thank you also to Richard Pike at C+W for his encouragement with this project and for helping me see the bigger picture.

I would like to thank Natasha Dow Schull, Young-Hoon Oh and Duncan Stibbard Hawkes for being interviewed for this book, and sharing their academic work in a way that is (I hope) accessible beyond anthropology.

Somewhat appropriately, writing a book about endurance – particularly one that involves participation in endurance events, with young children at home – has been something of an ultramarathon in itself. Above all, I therefore thank Roslyn, without whom it would not have been possible.

INDEX

INDEX